Memories of the Southern Civil Rights Movement

The Marx Building on Raymond Street in Atlanta, headquarters of SNCC in 1963, as it appears today

Memories of the Southern Civil Rights Movement

Danny Lyon

With a Foreword by Julian Bond

The Lyndhurst Series on the South
Published for the Center for Documentary Studies, Duke University,
by The University of North Carolina Press,
Chapel Hill and London

This is the second in a series of five books on the South supported by the Lyndhurst Foundation of Chattanooga, Tennessee. Alex Harris, Series Editor.

Design by Guy Russell and Danny Lyon
Type set by Kristopher Hill/FinalCopy
© 1992 The University of North Carolina Press
Photographs © 1992 by Danny Lyon
All rights reserved
Reproduction rights to the photographs of Danny Lyon are available from the Magnum Photos Archive, New York, N.Y.
Printed in Japan
96 95 94 93 92   5 4 3 2 1

Memories of the Southern Civil Rights Movement was designed and composed using PageMaker 4.2 on a Macintosh IIci with a SuperMac 19" color monitor and Spectrum/24 Series III video board. The original documents were scanned at 600dpi with a Hewlett-Packard ScanJet Plus. The text typeface is Adobe Systems' Monotype Bembo; titling is Adobe Systems' ITC Stone Serif. The paper in this book meets the guidelines for permanence and durability of the Committee on Production Guidelines for Book Longevity of the Council on Library Resources.

Library of Congress Cataloging-in-Publication Data

Lyon, Danny.
  Memories of the Southern civil rights movement / text and photographs by Danny Lyon ; foreword by Julian Bond.
    p. cm.—(The Lyndhurst series on the South)
  Includes bibliographical references (p.).
  ISBN 0-8078-2054-7 (alk. paper).—ISBN 0-8078-4386-5 (pbk. : alk. paper)
  1. Afro-Americans—Civil rights—Southern States. 2. Afro-Americans—Civil rights—Southern States—Pictorial works. 3. Civil rights movements—Southern States—History—20th century. 4. Civil rights movements—Southern States—History—20th century—Pictorial works. 5. Southern States—Race relations. 6. Lyon, Danny. 7. Civil rights workers—Southern States—Biography.
I. Title. II. Series.
E185.615L96 1992
323'.0975—dc20
                                                                                    92-5961
                                                                                         CIP

Contents

Foreword by Julian Bond   *6*

"We Happy Few," 1955–1961   *8*

Cairo, Illinois, 1962   *22*

Albany, Georgia, August 1962   *28*

Mississippi, September 1962   *38*

Nashville, November 1962: The Annual SNCC Conference   *48*

Mississippi, 1963   *54*

Winona, Mississippi, June 9, 1963   *56*

Danville, Virginia, June 10, 1963   *62*

Gadsden, Alabama, June 1963   *70*

Savannah, Georgia   *72*

The Leesburg, Georgia, Stockade   *78*

Washington, D.C., August 28, 1963   *82*

Birmingham, Alabama, September 12, 1963   *88*

Selma, October 7, 1963   *98*

Mississippi, Fall 1963   *104*

Southwest Georgia, 1963   *114*

Atlanta, November 22, 1963   *118*

Atlanta, Winter 1963–1964   *124*

Hattiesburg, Mississippi, January 22, 1964   *130*

Cambridge, Maryland, Spring 1964   *136*

Atlanta, June 10, 1964: Staff Meeting   *142*

Mississippi Summer, 1964   *148*

The Waveland Conference, November 1964   *162*

Montgomery, March 7, 1965   *166*

Peg Leg Bates, Kerhonkson, N.Y., December 1966   *174*

Trinity College, Hartford, Connecticut, April 1989: Epilogue   *182*

Sources   *186*

Acknowledgments   *192*

Foreword

Danny Lyon took pictures for the Student Nonviolent Coordinating Committee (SNCC) from 1962 until 1964.

The southern United States were in turmoil. In 1954 *Brown* v. *Board of Education* had destroyed segregation's legality; in 1955 in Montgomery, a nonviolent army quickly arose to challenge its morality as well. The student sit-ins of 1960 had spread from Greensboro, North Carolina, across the South, and the predominately youthful Freedom Rides of 1961 had shown the world the brave determination of the integrationists and the angry hatred of the white supremacists who opposed them. By 1962 the movement was regrouping; it was losing some of its spontaneity, digging into Albany in southwest Georgia, Selma, Alabama, and rural Mississippi, establishing bases in black communities, planning for the long haul.

Danny Lyon was twenty, SNCC was two. He was as idealistic as the rest of us. Someone in SNCC called him "Dandelion" because his curly hair resembled that flower. Inquisitive, New York-y, rumpled, he joined the band of brothers and circle of trust as the first of several fine photographers who documented, recorded, and froze the movement and its supporters and opponents into black and white. He had been hooked by the bravery of SNCC's John Lewis and the simplicity of SNCC's style. His SNCC-time is a snapshot of the organization that thought itself the radical wing of the nonviolent southern movement; the people, faces, and places seen here capture the heat and excitement and despair of those two hopeful years.

SNCC's idea of photography was functional: it was to provide pictures for SNCC's propaganda and for press releases to those papers that would print them, and it was used to illustrate fund-raising brochures and to document the movement.

Danny Lyon took this function and made art.

The young people who worked for SNCC described themselves as organizers. They didn't register voters—they organized the unregistered to register themselves. They didn't integrate lunch counters—they organized a protest that forced the seats open. They didn't integrate America—they showed what an integrated America could be like.

Lyon's pictures became organizers as well. They silently spoke words and conveyed emotions that speakers could not. But in the two years he worked to produce organizing art, the band of brothers and circle of trust began to come undone. By the time Lyon left SNCC in 1964, the two years he had photographed must have seemed like twenty.

Danny Lyon flew to Birmingham in 1963 in time to photograph the smoke rising from the bombed ruins of the Sixteenth Street Baptist Church where four little girls died. He sneaked behind a rural southwest Georgia jail to photograph young teenagers crowded into filth. Policemen gave him the finger; some barely let him escape a beating or worse. He was at the March on Washington, recording the dream some members of the throng saw, not just the dream some of the speakers promised. He took pictures in the summer of 1964 along some of the same roads traveled by Andy Goodman, Mickey Schwerner, and James Chaney. He photographed the endless staff meetings where race became reason against instead of reason for. He spent time behind bars. And he saw and recorded the movement: the people who made it, those who would maim and kill to stop it, and those who watched—respectfully, resentfully, or angrily—as it passed by.

Twenty-year-old Danny Lyon and the two-year-old Student Nonviolent Coordinating Committee were an improbable match. SNCC was born of the 1960 sit-in demonstrations by southern black college youth, who were tired of the slow pace of desegregation and worried that America's apartheid would cheapen their educations, rendering them useless. Danny Lyon matched most of these student rebels in age and outlook, if not in race, but rage against the old ways united him and them in common cause. Lyon traveled directly from his graduation from the University of Chicago to the all-black hospital in Danville, Virginia, making a fluent transition from academic confirmation to racial confrontation. SNCC's young people were organized anarchists, railing against both the segregated system and the slow-but-sure legal tactics used by older organizations to bring it down. Lyon was a rebel too— against unthinking order and despotic authority.

Photographer and sponsor became a perfect fit. These photos, many published here for the first time, are the result of that collaboration. They give today's audience a view lacking in scholarly accounts of the movement. Here are the faces and the bodies caught in action and emotion. Here is a true picture—not just photographs— of the movement and its promise. That promise failed. Danny Lyon's work is pictures both of what was and of what might have been.

The civil rights movement is much remembered and celebrated today. My students have a television picture of the movement in their minds: grainy black-and-white footage taken at the March on Washington or in Birmingham, dramatic moments from a movement whose reality appears much sharper and more clearly here. Dusty roads were the movement's most likely location, not Capitol malls and monuments. We all remember fire hoses and police dogs. Danny Lyon makes us remember the people and the forgotten places, too.

—*Julian Bond*

"We Happy Few," 1955–1961

Campaign posters near Atlanta today

Throughout the 1950s, the entire American South was segregated. African Americans were kept away from whites by law. Blacks could not eat in restaurants with whites. They could only ride in the backs of buses and had to give up their seats to whites if the buses were full. Movie theaters were segregated. So were public beaches and libraries. By law, blacks were kept in all-black schools, and in almost every way these schools were much poorer than the white schools. Black families on the road had to find a colored motel or a colored bathroom in order to stop, or they simply had to sleep in the car or keep on driving. This was the situation in all of the southern states when I was a high school student in New York City in the late 1950s. My own high school had 4,000 students, 90 percent of whom were Jewish and two of whom were black.*

In 1955 a black seamstress named Rosa Parks refused to give up her seat to a white on a crowded Montgomery, Alabama, bus. Among the people she worked for at the time were Clifford and Virginia Durr. When a scholarship became available for a short trip to the Highlander Folk School, a progressive school in Tennessee, Virginia Durr suggested that Rosa Parks take it. She did, and three weeks after her return from Highlander, Rosa Parks refused to move from her seat when ordered to do so and was arrested. Within days, thousands of Negroes in Montgomery refused to ride the buses, beginning a boycott that went on for over a year. Initially the boycott was led by E. D. Nixon, a railroad porter and disciple of A. Philip Randolph. Then a group of ministers formed the Montgomery Improvement Association and picked as its leader a new minister from Atlanta, Dr. Martin Luther King, Jr. They chose King partly because he was new in town, and partly because his diction was good and northerners would be able to understand him. (As SNCC workers would later joke, they picked King and got "de Lawd.") The death knell was starting to sound for legal segregation, a direct descendant of slavery and of the whole unhappy history of Americans brought here in chains from across the ocean. In African American communities across the South, men and women, students and children, were about to do for themselves what no one else had ever done and no one else could do.

> We few, we happy few, we band of brothers
> For he today that sheds his blood with me
> Shall be my brother.

Fifty miles from Montgomery, a young Alabama man heard of the boycott by listening to the radio. Living on his parents' farm, he went to a small rural school populated mostly by his cousins and spent a lot of his time caring for the family's chickens, to which he was deeply attached. He spoke to the chickens and gave them names and dreaded when one would be slaughtered for dinner, which he then refused to eat. He never saw white people, for none were around, and one of his fondest wishes was for an incubator that he had seen in the Sears, Roebuck catalog, hopelessly out of reach at a price of $29.00. He wanted to be the first black to attend the local school, Troy State College, so he took a bus to Montgomery to meet his new hero, Dr. King, and both King and Ralph Abernathy were astounded that this young rural person, still a teenager, would take what seemed a suicidal task upon himself. John Lewis

---

*During the writing of this book, black was still in popular usage. It is currently being replaced by African American, and I have used both words throughout the text. A generation ago, when the pictures were being made, use of the words Negro and colored was common both within and outside the movement. I have also used those words at times because I did not wish too often to impose the present upon the past.

was, in fact, too young to sue the state of Alabama to allow him to enter Troy State, and his parents refused to do it and bring the danger upon themselves. So instead he went to Nashville to attend the American Baptist Theological Seminary, which was free. In order to support himself there, he washed dishes at the school.

In 1969 Archie Allen tape-recorded John Lewis's memories of his life:

> *Lewis*: My father had saved enough money to buy 100 acres of land with a very old house on it, with a tin top. We moved in that house when I was four years old.
> *Allen*: What kind of farm did you have?
> *Lewis*: Tenant … rented … the man furnished the land. Maybe it was rented, I guess. The man furnished the land and the house. We had to pay a certain percentage of the produce.
> *Allen*: What was the produce?
> *Lewis*: Cotton, corn, and peanuts. The house was located right on the … right beside a dirt road. And I remember that very, very well, 'cause that's when I first started baptizing chickens, when I was three and four years old. During that period I became very, very fond of chickens.

When John Lewis went off to Nashville in the late 1950s, he joined a group of people who were about to make history. Diane Nash was a beauty queen from Chicago and a student at Fisk University. Bernard Lafayette, also at Fisk, had arrived from Tampa. Marion Barry, Angie Butler, and Paul LaPrad were there, as was James Bevel, a preacher from Dickerson, Tennessee. What brought them all together in Nashville were workshops in nonviolence being taught by Jim Lawson on Monday nights. Lawson, a minister and follower of Gandhi (he had gone to prison rather than serve in the Korean War), was training a small group of students to make a nonviolent revolution. In the fall of 1959, the group tried a "test" sit-in at a segregated Harvey's in Nashville. That Christmas when they went home, John Lewis and his new friend, Bernard Lafayette, sat in the front of the bus and rode it together to Atlanta, and then John stayed there all the way back to Troy, a violation of local law and custom. On Monday, February 1, 1960, four students sat in on their own in a Greensboro, North Carolina, Woolworth's lunch counter. On Tuesday, the number of students who sat in at the Woolworth's quadrupled, and on Wednesday the number quadrupled again. The sit-ins in Greensboro were like a bell in the night. Diane Nash and Lawson's students quickly organized others to sit in across Nashville, and within two months nonviolent demonstrations against segregation had erupted throughout the city. John Lewis was asked to write a list of "do's and don'ts" to instruct the increasing numbers who were joining the protests. The Nashville Code became the guide for all the sit-ins to follow.

1. Don't strike back or curse if abused.
2. Don't laugh out.
3. Don't hold conversations with floor workers.
4. Don't block entrances to the stores and aisles.
5. Show yourself courteous and friendly at all times.
6. Sit straight and always face the counter.
7. Remember love and nonviolence.
8. May God bless each of you.

Arrests came quickly as the sit-ins spread. "It was a great feeling really" is how John Lewis described passing through the middle-class trauma of breaking the law. A band of brothers and sisters was being formed, for many of the people present at the very beginning of the movement would be there to guide it forward for another five and six years. Some of them would shed their blood before it was over, and during the course of the movement at least thirty would die.

By April 1960, sit-ins had occurred in 125 southern cities. In May all of the downtown lunch counters in Nashville were integrated. It was a stupendous victory for the students. Although they did not know it at the time, the Nashville student movement, led by Diane Nash and Bernard Lafayette and guided by Jim Lawson's teachings, had inaugurated a period of revolt and rebellion in America that would not come to an end for fifteen years. For in 1961, even as the movement spread across the South, John F. Kennedy, the new American president, was sending the first military men to southeast Asia in a move that would see the United States take the place of France as a colonial ruler in South Vietnam. Blacks revolted first against oppression and discrimination in the South, and that revolt, which was largely successful in achieving its initial aims, continued for six years. Then the revolt spread to masses of young white Americans, although the issue that united them in rebellion was not injustices against blacks at home but the injustice of a colonial war that was killing black and white Americans alike, not to mention untold hundreds of thousands of Asians. One might say that the southern civil rights movement was the first half of a great rebellion that almost brought a revolution to America.

As the sit-ins continued in Nashville restaurants, James Bevel and John Lewis were almost gassed to death when they went into a Krystal's by themselves. Again from Allen's interview with Lewis:

> *Lewis*: The fumigating machine was placed on and we were fumigated. We started coughing and sneezing and the fumes just sort of clouded up everything. We couldn't see outside. We heard a fire engine and I believe a fireman came up and knocked on the door. Then the manager opened up the door and let us out.
> *Allen*: Couldn't you turn off the machine?
> *Lewis*: I don't think so. I never thought of it. I don't think there was any feeling on my part to interfere with the machine.
> *Allen*: The manager stated that it was a state law to fumigate. What was your impression at that point?
> *Lewis*: I had a . . . really, I had a strange feeling. I thought maybe we'd just be there and . . . then I kept on saying, "No, the man couldn't let us die in here. He wouldn't do that." All types of things were going throughout my mind. "He wouldn't do that. How could he explain that he'd let us die in here?"

In April 1960, Jim Lawson had been conducting his workshops in Nashville on Monday nights for eighteen months. But many people in the black community had been awaiting the revolt for years. To the students, the most important of these people was a diminutive woman named Ella Baker. She did not see the sit-ins as the pivotal event that my generation would because she had been involved in the struggle for black liberation her entire life. Others had worked for twenty or thirty years through the NAACP and through the courts toward the same ends that the students were now so quickly achieving. But Baker immediately grasped the significance of what

Ella Baker, who called the 1960 meeting of student activists in Raleigh, North Carolina, that created SNCC

the sit-ins had started. Using $800 that she received from the Southern Christian Leadership Conference, the civil rights organization of southern ministers led by Dr. King, she called a meeting in Raleigh, North Carolina, to bring together the students who were active in sit-ins across the South. One hundred and twenty-five were expected; three hundred came. The SCLC immediately tried to control the student group, but Ella Baker warned against it, and adult leadership was rejected.

Nineteen northern schools were represented at the conference, and these students raised a problem that would dog the history of the movement. They had "a great urge to be identified with the southern movement," John Lewis recalled. Some of the southerners had come straight from jail and were recognized heroes and heroines. The northerners, mostly white and often more articulate politically than the southerners, had to be kept from overwhelming the very students whose actions they so admired. In order to keep southern control of the movement, separate meetings of southern and northern students were held. Ella Baker, who along with Lawson and King addressed the entire group, was about to become midwife to one of the most effective grass-roots organizations in our history. Ever mindful of an unspoiled birth, she suggested that the press be excluded. The initial name of the new group of southern students was the Continuations Committee, and Marion Barry of the Nashville movement was chosen as chairman. Each state was to have one or two representatives. They agreed to meet again in the fall in Atlanta, and in June, Jane Stembridge, a young white poet and native Virginian, volunteered to be secretary. The Student Nonviolent Coordinating Committee (SNCC, pronounced "snick"), as it was soon renamed, now had one employee.

In 1961 John Lewis was elected president of the student body at the college where he had spent two years washing dishes, but he missed his senior sermon, which was required for graduation, because he was in jail. Students had been conducting stand-ins at segregated movie theaters, and by February the Nashville theaters had thrown in the towel and opened up to blacks. The title of Lewis's undelivered sermon was to be "I Bring Not Peace but a Sword." There is no question that Diane Nash intended the movement in just that way. At the August 1961 meeting of SNCC at the Highlander School in Tennessee, where Rosa Parks had been politicized six years earlier, the group almost split in two. At the time many thought that voter registration work would be less dangerous than direct confrontations against segregation, and the new group decided to work in both areas. Diane Nash was elected chairman for direct action and Charles Jones was elected chairman for voter registration. SNCC was going to take a no-compromise stance on all its issues and come at America with a moral sword. It was SNCC's greatest attraction and perhaps its greatest contribution to the following decade. SNCC's total rejection of American politics set a standard that movement after movement would, at their finest moments, aspire to as they followed in SNCC's wake.

When the first sit-ins occurred in Greensboro in February 1960, it was as if people had been waiting for them. Julian Bond, who was at Morehouse in Atlanta, describes himself then as "just an ordinary student." But he was waiting to follow someone who would take the first bold step to lead. When Lonnie King came to Julian and told him it was time to move, Julian did just that. His life would never be the same again.

Jane Stembridge (left), the Virginia native and poet who volunteered to be the first secretary of SNCC

Bond: Lonnie King was a student, he was an older guy; he had been in the Navy. He was not related to Martin Luther King but he had known Martin Luther King most of his life. He grew up in Ebenezzar Baptist Church. He was a church guy. He came to me one day, about February 3rd of 1960, with this newspaper, the *Atlantic Daily World,* and it said something like "Greensboro students sit in for third day." And he said, "What do you think about that?" and I said, "Gee, that's great." Then he said, "Do you think it ought to happen here?" and I said, "I'm sure it will happen here," and he said, "Why don't we make it happen here?" and I said, "What do you mean we?"

What Bond and Lonnie King did then was typical of the southern movement. They acted immediately, literally at that moment dividing up the cafeteria and going from group to group, organizing a meeting to start the sit-ins in Atlanta. Within a month almost two hundred black students from five Atlanta schools had been arrested. The one white teacher who immediately came to the aid and support of the students was Howard Zinn, who in 1964 would publish *SNCC: The New Abolitionists,* the first book-length account of the radical organization.

Bond: I took the group to the city hall, which was cafeteria style, you took a tray through, and we lined up. There was a heavy-set white woman who was in charge of the facility. "I'm sorry, you all can't eat here. This is for city hall employees."

I said, "Well, there's a big sign out front that says 'City Hall Cafeteria, the Public Is Welcome.' " And she said, "Well, we don't really mean it." So I said, "We'll just wait here till you serve us," and she said, "Well, I'm gonna call the police." And the police came and they arrested us, put us in a paddy wagon and took us down to the city jail which was called Big Rock. . . . And then about 8 o'clock that night adults in the community bonded us all out, and we went to Pasqual's for a celebration chicken dinner. We were heroes.

That April some Atlanta adults rented a large car so that seven or eight students could drive to Raleigh for the historic conference called by Ella Baker. Although the singing of freedom songs was always part of the Albany, Georgia, movement, none of the students in the first Atlanta sit-ins sang any songs at all. At the Raleigh conference they heard Guy Carawan sing a new version of an old labor song called "We Shall Overcome," which became the anthem of the southern civil rights movement. Movement people would join hands and almost go into a trance as they gently swayed back and forth singing "black and white together" and the chorus, "Deep in my heart, I do believe, / We shall overcome some day," over and over. It was a relief from the tensions and the dangers of the day and night, a literal coming together and reaching out to one another for support.

At first SNCC had only a single windowless room in the SCLC office, with Jane Stembridge the only person working in it. In the summer of 1960, Bob Moses, a high school math teacher from Harlem, came south and went to the SCLC office to help "lick stamps." He and Jane Stembridge became friends. When a student meeting was held in the fall, only a few came from Alabama and none came from Mississippi at all. So Bob Moses went to the Mississippi home of NAACP leader Amzie Moore, a Delta black who, like Ella Baker, had been fighting for his people's

```
                    ROCK  HILL,  SOUTH  CAROLINA

ROCK HILL,S.C.—Feb. 20...Eight Negro students jailed in a Rock Hill, S. C.,
"SIT-IN" demonstration have been placed on BREAD AND WATER in solitary confine-
ment for what prison officials called a sit down and refusal to work.  In a
special interview with the Rev. C. A. Ivory, president of the York County chapter
of the NAACP, SNCC learned that the 11 students serving 30 day sentences for a
"SIT-IN" were being told to load 36 loads of dirt on a truck each day, and the
other crew were being made to 32 loads of dirt with a 27 man working force.  The
students objected to this as being unfair and sat down in protest to the conditions.

                    SUMTER,  SOUTH  CAROLINA

SUMTER, S.C.—Feb.22...Police broke up an anti-segregation march Tuesday with
wholesale arrest of young Negroes who refused orders to turn back to the Morris
College campus.  At nightfall, 65 Negroes were in jail, charged with breach of
the peace.  Sit-In demonstrations at Lawson's and Alderman's Drug stores and at
the Carnegie Public Library also resulted in some arrests during the day.  But
most arrest came during the march.  The students, many of whom sang hymns, made
no immediate effort to raise money to meet the $100 bond set for each.  A Negro
cook, Mae Frances Moultrie, of Atlanta, Ga., claimed she was roughed up by a
policeman, resulting in her hospitalization.

                    COLUMBIA,  SOUTH  CAROLINA

COLUMBIA,S.C.—Feb.22...An estimated 70 Negro college students carried anti-
segregation signs and staged "SIT-IN" demonstrations at White lunch counters
in downtown Columbia.  Five of the students tried to walk past a no trespassing
sign toward a lunch counter at Eckerd's Drug store and were promptly arrested
and charged with trespassing. Jailed while attempts were made to raise bonds of
$100 each  were Benedict College students Joseph B. Bailey, Joan Brailey, Carolyn
Montgomery, Clifford James Rice and David Green.  Seven other Benedict students
were arrested Tuesday at Eskerd's on identical charges.  The student leader,
David Carter of Benedict College, has said such demonstrations will occur here
"indefinitely".

COLUMBIA,S.C.—The SNCC office learned monday that the Greyhound Corporation's
terminal at Columbia has quietly dropped segregation at the lunch counter.
```

(Above) One of SNCC's earliest news releases
(Left) Julian Bond, a SNCC publicist and student activist from Atlanta. Bond was later elected to the Georgia state legislature, and in 1968 his name was put in nomination as Democratic candidate for vice president of the United States (he was too young).

Robert Parris Moses, a New York City high school math teacher, led SNCC's struggle in Mississippi.

rights his whole life. He was about to get a lot of company. Ella Baker said, "The whole concept of SNCC was to deal with the hard-core areas." At the fall 1961 meeting, a number of students decided to drop out of school and "put their bodies on the line."

Many of them went with Bob Moses to McComb, Mississippi, one of the worst areas in the most racist state in the South. They were supposed to be working on voter registration. But in the reality of hot, rural southwestern Mississippi, they found that voter registration and direct action were pretty much the same thing. Local high school students, led by Brenda Travis and Curtis Hayes, marched out of the school. Bob Zellner, the lone white SNCC fieldworker from Alabama who was supposed to maintain a "low profile," instead joined the march. Zellner was assaulted. Later, Moses was assaulted. Travis and Hayes were expelled from school. Everyone was arrested. Sitting in jail in Magnolia, Moses, the New York mathematics teacher, composed a letter that became a movement legend. With vision and more than a touch of romance, he describes his cellmates and envisions a great change coming to the South. The racist laws of Mississippi that had held African Americans down since Reconstruction were about to be overthrown.

November 1, 1961

I am writing this note from the drunk tank of the county jail in Magnolia, Mississippi. Twelve of us are here, sprawled out along the concrete bunker: C. Curtis Hayes, Hollis Watkins, Ike Lewis, and Robert Talbert, four veterans of the bunker, are sitting up talking—mostly about girls: McDew ("Tell the story") is curled into the concrete and the wall; Harold Robinson, Stephen Ashley, James Wells, Lee Chester Vick, Leetus Eubanks, and Ivory Diggs lay cramped on the cold bunker; I'm sitting with smuggled pen and paper, thinking a little, writing a little; Myrtis Bennett and Janie Campbell are across the way, wedded to a different icy cubicle.

Later on Hollis will lead out with a clear tenor into a freedom song. Talbert and Lewis will supply jokes, and McDew will discourse on the history of the black man and the Jew. McDew, a black by birth, a Jew by choice, and a revolutionary by necessity, has taken the deep hates and loves of America, and the world, reserved for those who dare to stand in a strong sun and cast a sharp shadow.

In the words of Judge Brumfield, who sentenced us, we are "cold calculators" who design to disrupt the racial harmony (harmonious since 1619) of McComb into racial strife and rioting; we, he said, are the leaders who are causing young children to be led like sheep to the pen to be slaughtered (in a legal manner). "Robert," he was addressing me, "haven't some of the people from your school been able to go down and register without violence here in Pike County?" I thought to myself that Southerners are exposed the most, when they boast.

It's mealtime now: we have rice and gravy in a flat pan, dry bread and a "big town cake"; we lack eating and drinking utensils. Water comes from a faucet and goes into a hole.

This is Mississippi, the middle of the iceberg. Hollis is leading off with his tenor, "Michael row the boat ashore, Alleluia; Christian brothers don't be slow, Alleluia; Mississippi next to go, Alleluia." This is a tremor in the middle of the iceberg—from a stone that the builders rejected.

Bob Moses

The people who joined Moses were themselves inspired by friends who had taken the Freedom Rides that had begun four months earlier. Moses later credited the Freedom Rides with giving the voter registration workers in McComb an identity. Before, he and his associates had been nameless. Now, in Mississippi, they were called "Freedom Riders."

The rides were initiated by the Congress of Racial Equality, a radical civil rights organization whose roots went back to a pacifist movement during World War II, when one of its most active members, Bayard Rustin, served time in Lewisburg Penitentiary for refusing to serve in the armed forces. As early as 1947, CORE had sponsored a Freedom Ride through the segregated South. Led by James Farmer, CORE fieldworkers in the South often marched with and were jailed alongside SNCC workers. (During one of the grimmest moments of the movement, workers recruited by both organizations would be murdered and buried together.) In May 1961, two buses sponsored by CORE began their ride across the South to test interstate facilities that were supposed to be integrated according to federal law. John Lewis, who was one of two SNCC students and, at twenty-one, the youngest person on the ride, was punched in the face as he tried to use the bathroom at the Greyhound station in Rock Hill, South Carolina. In Anniston, Alabama, one bus was bombed and burned. The other bus was attacked by a mob in Birmingham, and James Peck, who had spent three years in prison for his beliefs, was hospitalized with fifty stitches in his face. At that point, CORE canceled the rides because it felt they were just too dangerous. But Diane Nash and other members of the Nashville movement insisted that the rides go on.

The Nashville student leadership, meeting around the clock, displayed what was becoming a normal characteristic of those in the movement: the ability to act almost immediately once having decided on a course of action. The problem wasn't recruiting riders—it was obtaining the blessing of the adult clerical community so that the students could get the funds to buy the bus tickets. On a Wednesday night, the bus was bombed in Anniston and the rides were canceled by CORE. On Sunday morning, after several days and nights of nonstop debate and activity, the new recruits rolled out of Nashville and into history. Among them were James Zwerg, Selyn McCollum, Paul Brooks, Lucretia Collins, and again John Lewis, the only person to be on both legs of the ride. In Montgomery a mob of one thousand people attacked the defenseless riders. There is a picture of John Lewis standing alongside Jim Zwerg as Zwerg searches inside his bloody mouth for missing teeth. Both are neatly dressed in jackets and ties, their white shirts spattered with their own blood.

Taylor Branch's detailed account of this event, included in the first volume of his work on Martin Luther King, Jr., belongs on the school desk of every American ten-year-old. It is a story of absolute courage—of American women and men, black

Bob Zellner (above)
(Left) John Lewis in Nashville

James Forman, author and organizer, executive secretary of SNCC from 1961 to 1966, SNCC's most successful years

and white, Jewish, Catholic, and Protestant, literally ready to die for the ideas that this country has always claimed it stood for but in its history has hardly ever actually practiced. Later Nash said that if she and her colleagues had let violence stop the rides, the movement would have been finished. It wasn't finished. For the many who would go south, the civil rights movement was born in the blood and flames through which these two dozen young men and women passed.

When the SNCC staff still numbered only three people—Jane Stembridge, Norma Collins, and John Hardy—James Forman, a former Chicago schoolteacher and publicist, arrived in Atlanta to write articles about the new student movement and stayed. Forman, an Air Force veteran who had been raised partly in Mississippi and had served in a segregated Air Force, was ten years older than most of the other members. When fifteen people arrived from the field for the first staff meeting, many from McComb, Forman gave in to pressure from them to remain in the office and keep SNCC running while the others returned to the field. Bob Moses was so anxious to return to McComb that he had to be argued into staying at the meeting one extra day. Charles McDew, still in McComb, didn't even come to the meeting.

Like many in the movement, Forman would rather have been doing other things that he thought he was better at—"agitating, organizing, or writing." Despite that, as first executive secretary Forman built SNCC into an organization that led a mass movement in the South and then guided it through its most successful years. One of his first acts was to bring Julian Bond, whose file said he was an Atlanta journalism student, on to the staff. Then he hired Bob Zellner.

Following is an excerpt from a letter written by Tom Hayden, then editor of the newspaper at the University of Michigan at Ann Arbor, to Al Haber, president of the Students for a Democratic Society, in September 1961. Hayden briefly reports on the Freedom Rides, mentioning that he thinks Klan members from six states took part in the Montgomery attack, and on a SNCC meeting that fall. Harry Belafonte has provided some funds to SNCC, and now seventeen people are on the staff. Some of the names he mentions—Bob Moses, Reggie Robinson, McArthur Cotton, Jim Travis, Charles Sherrod, Chuck McDew—will appear again and again in this story.

McDew later said that as the students from various colleges, drawn originally by the sit-ins, gathered together in SNCC, they made a decision to leave school and devote five years of their lives to the movement. Many of them were children of the middle class who had to face incredulous or horrified parents back home. Others had parents who knew exactly why their sons or daughters were leaving comfortable homes to venture into the rural South and who supported them. Of those who survived the five years, all were completely altered by the experience.

Encouraged by Forman, Tom Hayden had also been drawn to the South. In the final paragraph of his letter to Haber, he predicts with keen foresight the course of American history for the next decade. Part journalist, part activist, Hayden followed Moses and the SNCC workers to McComb. There, as he drove along with Paul Potter, he was dragged from the car by a white in a sleeveless sweatshirt and clubbed over the head. A local photographer in the following car got out and took a photograph as Hayden crouched on the ground, trying to cover his head and ward off the blows.

"That picture made me famous," Hayden said recently.

I was nineteen years old and beginning my third year as a student at the University of Chicago when I saw that photograph reproduced in the student paper, *The Maroon*. I was also a photographer, a history student, and an admirer of Mathew Brady, "the historian with a camera." If Tom Hayden could go from Michigan to Mississippi, why couldn't I? At the end of that school year, with an army bag holding two cameras, I had my sister-in-law drive me out to old Route 66, because that is the road Jack Kerouac used. Then I stuck out my thumb and headed south.

Bob Moses

A year after the Freedom Rides, segregation signs still stand outside the Jackson, Mississippi, bus terminal.

Most important is the crazy new sentiment that this is not a movement but a revolution, that our identity should be not with our Negro predecessors but with the new nations around the world, and that beyond lunch counter desegregation there are more serious evils which must be ripped out by any means: exploitation, socially destructive capital, evil political and legal structure, and myopic liberalism which is anti-revolutionary. Revolution permeates discussion like never before; I presume it was the Nashville seminar more than anything else which provided the opportunity for changing the thrust of the movement. In our future dealings we should be aware that they have changed down there, and we should speak their revolutionary language without mocking it, for it is not lip service, nor is it the ego fulfillment of a rising Negro class, but it is in truth the fact of life in the South this minute, and unless the North or the government or the nuclear war intervene, we are going to be down there soon ourselves in jail, or fighting, or writing, or being lynched in the struggle. It is a good pure struggle, the kind that can bring hope to Africans and Asians and the rest of the hungry peoples, and it is a struggle that we have every reason to begin in a revolutionary way across the country, in every place of discrimination that exists. There is no reason for us to be hesitant anymore. There is no reason for us to fear that the civil rights movement is degenerate. There is no reason for us to think we can do something "more important out of jail." Two years ago we falsified this movement to claim it was the event with which we identified. We didn't. We saw it as something that we should extend, that we could both help in justice to ourselves and which could at the same time provide a cutting edge for more reforms throughout the society. Well, now the Southern movement has turned itself into that revolution we hoped for, and we didn't have much to do with its turning at all. The Southern students did, and Tim Jenkins did, and Belafonte a little bit. But mostly the Southern students. And now they are miles ahead of us, looking back, chuckling knowingly about the sterility of liberals, tightening grimly against the potency of the racists. In the rural South, in the "token integration" areas, in the cities, they will be shouting from the bottom of their guts for justice or else. We had better be there.

The final paragraph of a letter written by Tom Hayden to SDS president Al Haber in September 1961

Cairo, Illinois, 1962

In the summer of 1962, I was putting a spark plug into my 650cc Triumph motorcycle. Completely inept as a mechanic, I tried to force the spark plug into the soft aluminum head and stripped the threads inside the engine. Until that moment, riding my motorcycle through the streets of the South Side had been my major occupation. Despite my abuse, my motorcycle had always kept running. Now it was disabled. Linda Pearlstein, a fellow student at the University of Chicago, had been in demonstrations in Cairo, Illinois, and had been arrested there. With contacts obtained from her, I took my Nikon F camera and some bulk-loaded film and hitchhiked from Chicago to Cairo, 390 miles south at the confluence of the Mississippi and Ohio rivers. This town once marked the spot between freedom and slavery across the river in Missouri. Cairo was the town that Huckleberry Finn and the runaway slave Jim were heading to on their raft but sailed by in the night. I missed it also. I ended up in East St. Louis and made a call from a phone booth to tell Selyn McCollum that I would be arriving later by bus. Everything was very cloak-and-dagger. As I stepped off the bus in the night, the person who came toward me was the tall Chico Neblett, then from behind him stepped Selyn. I was given a place to stay and breakfast by people I had never even met before.

On June 7, 1962, John Lewis had written to James Forman and Chuck McDew in Atlanta offering to work for SNCC for the summer and asking if they could send the $10.00 he needed to make the trip up from his home in Troy, Alabama. Norma Collins, who was now working in the Atlanta office, sent him a check for $10.00 and added, "as Jim put it to me, 'come home.'" John offered to join a group in Mt. Vernon, but instead he was sent north, to Cairo, Illinois.

Route 5 Box 225
Troy, Alabama
June 7 1962

Mr James Forman & Charles McDew.
Student Nonviolent Coordinating Comm.
135 Auburn Ave. N. E.
Atlanta 3, Georgia

Dear Chuck and Jim:
Will one of you make or get someone to make the Necessary Contact for Gadsden, Ala. I will be ready to go to Gadsden as soon as I receive the Necessary information and a small subsistence to take care of Transportation.
Look fellows I want to make it clear that I am at your disposal this summer. If I can be useful for anything let me know.
If you don't have someone to

to Mt. Vernon, I will be very happy to be a member of the group.
If it is all possible, send the information right away. Probably it would be wise to send the money in the form of a money order instead of a check. It might be hard to get a check Cash.
Did you get in Contact with Bernard LoFayette?
I think the Meeting was great. Hoping that everything is going Well. I hope also that we will soon be over and out of that $10,000 debt.
your For Freedom
John Lewis

I am writing this letter in a real hurry so I can drop it off before the mailman on his pick up.

The first time I saw John Lewis he was sitting quietly, bored or dreaming, in the back of a church in Cairo. Charles Koen, a high school student and movement leader, was speaking. Then John came to the podium. I had seldom been in a church before and had never heard a black preacher. The speech, delivered in a heavy, rural Alabama accent, seemed to come up out of him, out of centuries of abuse, and explode from this unassuming young man. His voice was high pitched and trembling with emotion. John's speech would have converted anyone, and it converted me. Then when he was done, he and Charles Koen led the small group out of the church and into the street to demonstrate. This was mind boggling because in 1962, while northern students often talked and argued about doing things, I never knew them to actually do anything.

Demonstrations at an "all-white" swimming pool in Cairo, Illinois

25

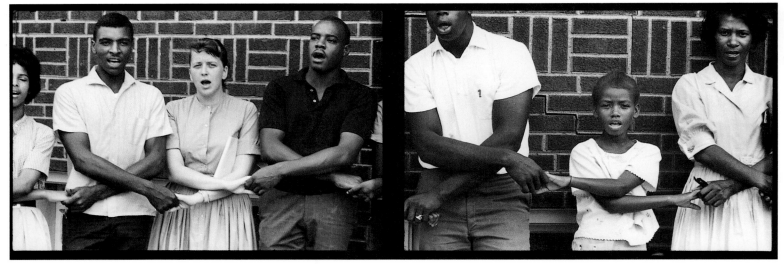

SNCC field secretaries Chico Neblett and Selyn McCollum (who had been a Freedom Rider) demonstrate at the Cairo pool. Second from the right is the girl who won't move for the truck.

It is hard to convey what this demonstration was like except by contrasting it with what we have been conditioned to expect today. There was no press, no video cameras (of course), no film cameras, no police, and no reporters. I had my camera, and I ran along as this brave little group marched through the sunlit and mostly empty streets of a very small American town. With the exception of a few young black men, everyone else who was watching seemed to hate and deride the demonstrators, many of whom were children. At Cairo's only, and segregated, swimming pool, the group stopped to pray. Then they stood in the street singing, and when a blue pickup truck drove down the center of the street straight at them, a game of chicken ensued as the truck slowed and the demonstrators moved out of the way, except for one defiant thirteen-year-old girl, who stood her ground until the truck knocked her down.

come let us build a new world together

STUDENT NONVIOLENT COORDINATING COMMITTEE 8½ RAYMOND STREET, N.W. ATLANTA 14, GEORGIA

A year after I made this photograph of John Lewis in Cairo, SNCC printed 10,000 copies of it as a poster and sold them for a dollar each, mostly in the North.

John Lewis speaks in a small Cairo church as high school leader Charles Koen watches. It is my first view of the Freedom Rider, future chairman of SNCC, and now U.S. congressman from Georgia.

The local police

Albany, Georgia
August 1962

On a hot August night, a mass meeting packs the Shiloh Baptist Church in Albany, Georgia.

Wyette T. Walker of the SCLC

From Cairo I went south to the small SNCC office in Atlanta. I recall standing by a highway and yelling up to ask the bus driver if he went to Milan, Tennessee, only he couldn't understand me. I kept saying "Milan" and the driver kept saying, "What?" Finally he said, "Oh, you mean *My*-lan," and I got on board. When I reached the Atlanta office, it was empty. In August 1962 everyone was in Albany, another 150 miles farther south. So I got on another bus, and since deciding where to sit was in effect a political statement, I stood. Near me was another standing passenger, a very smartly dressed man with glasses and a goatee. He said if I was going to try to reach the SNCC people, I ought to do it in the daylight and not at night. Police, in and out of uniform, stood around the parking lot as the bus pulled into Albany. As soon as I stepped off the bus, I was pulled aside by a plainclothesman. "Where you going?" I was asked. "That's the white part of town," he said and pointed, "and that's the nigger part of town." Wyette T. Walker, the gentleman I had been speaking with, walked off in one direction and I went off in the other.

In the morning I walked over to the black side of town to find the Albany movement. A year earlier, two people from the newly formed SNCC had arrived in Albany. Charles Sherrod, a divinity student from Virginia, and Cordell Reagon, a teenager and Freedom Rider from Nashville, had spent the first week playing basketball and letting the community get a good look at them. Their presence sparked action by local students, which in turn galvanized the entire community. The middle class of the black community had come together with ordinary workers and the students. Charles Sherrod and Cordell Reagon were able to take rival black street gangs that had been fighting each other and turn them into civil rights activists. Often the gang members were among the most courageous of the young activists. Two churches, Shiloh Baptist and Mt. Zion, located right across the street from each other, became the heart of the Albany movement, and Albany, Georgia, previously best known as the birthplace of Ray Charles, became one of the first and most powerful centers of the civil rights movement.

Many of the SNCC staff were present that week in August, including the executive secretary, James Forman. Smoking a corncob pipe, drifting in and out of the southern accent he had picked up in Mississippi, he was serious, extremely polite, and always under pressure. Forman treated me like he treated most newcomers. He put me to work. "You got a camera? Go inside the courthouse. Down at the back they have a big water cooler for whites and next to it a little bowl for Negroes. Go in there and take a picture of that."

With Forman's blessing, I had found a place in the civil rights movement that I would occupy for the next two years. James Forman would direct me, protect me, and at times fight for a place for me in the movement. He is directly responsible for my pictures existing at all.

Julian Bond has described a time in Atlanta when he and Forman would watch Dr. King and the SCLC deposit "huge sacks of money" in the bank, money that was arriving in the mail, often for the sit-ins being carried out by students. Sometimes SNCC received nothing at all. At the time, Forman was able to get Dr. King to give SNCC a few hundred dollars each month. As a publicist Forman was singularly aware that SNCC needed "an image." To the watching world, SNCC was faceless. In the summer of 1963, John Lewis, with his Alabama background and unparalleled record of arrests and commitment, replaced Chuck McDew as chairman. For many in the North, Lewis would come to personify the student movement. My photographs—made because I had studied history, made because I loved to make them, made under direction from Forman and the office—were used to help create a public image for SNCC. Through SNCC and its support groups in the North (the Chicago Friends of SNCC was the largest of these), they traveled all across America and even around the world.

The picture I made of John Lewis in Cairo, praying next to the brave young girl, was turned into a poster by Mark Suckle at the Atlanta SNCC office. Ten thousand copies were printed and most were sent north. Albany was quiet when I was there, so two people went out and got arrested on my behalf. The picture of Eddie Brown, an ex-gang leader, being carried away by police with a look of beatific serenity on his face was reproduced in college papers and SNCC fund-raising flyers. A picture I made the next year in front of Leb's Restaurant in Atlanta, which showed seventeen-year-old Taylor Washington being arrested for the eighth time, eventually showed up in the former USSR on the front page of section two of *Pravda*, captioned "Police Brutality USA." My uncle Lazaar Henkin brought a copy back from the Soviet Union after a business trip there.

Segregated drinking fountains in the county courthouse in Albany, Georgia

A meeting in Mount Zion Baptist Church

Bill Hansen, head of SNCC's Pine Bluff, Arkansas, office, in Albany

A northern student in Mount Zion Baptist

Kathleen Conwell

Not every arrest advanced the cause of the movement. I was arrested that week in a downtown Albany bar. A blonde girl I had met at the Freedom House went there to drink beer with me in the middle of the afternoon. The more beer we drank, the more she kept announcing that she was married to a black man somewhere up north. I suggested that maybe she shouldn't say that so loudly. The few people seated at the bar all seemed to be turning toward our table. She kept talking louder about her marriage, adding that, as Peter had betrayed Jesus before the cock crowed three times, I, being a Jew, would no doubt also betray her. I remember the bright sunlight as we stepped from the bar into the street and the six plainclothes police coming at us like in a Western movie. Only it wasn't a movie. I was taken to the city jail, where I was fingerprinted and my camera taken from me, and I was locked up in a four-man cell. The police wanted to know more about the girl. I really didn't know much about her, I explained. They said I could be charged with the Mann Act for bringing an underage girl across the state lines for purposes of prostitution. (Actually, I was the one who was underage.)

From where I was I couldn't see the person in the next cell, but I could speak with him. He was a student from the Midwest who had been jailed during earlier demonstrations. In jail for over a month, he was afraid that the movement had forgotten about him. He was also on a hunger strike. I could look through the bars of my cell across to the Negro side of the jail. About fifty feet away, in a cell almost directly opposite mine, was Albany's most famous prisoner, Dr. Martin Luther King, Jr. But he wasn't in his cell; he was seated outside it on a bench, eating chicken. A white sheet had been placed over the bench like a tablecloth, and Dr. King was having the lunch someone had brought in for him. He was also being examined by a physician. It was my first look at the man whose name now graces high schools and avenues across America. Dr. King was a very popular figure in the black community of Albany, but I saw him through the eyes of a twenty-year-old student and SNCC supporter, and young people and many SNCC workers had a lot of problems with Dr. King.

Charles Sherrod, the leader of SNCC's effort in southwest Georgia

Ralph Allen taking an affidavit from Carolyn Daniels in Terrill County

A street in Albany

Dr. Martin Luther King, Jr., and Reverend Ralph Abernathy are escorted back to jail in Albany.

SNCC was striving for a permanent social and political revolution in Albany and in the whole South. Many SNCC workers believed that the movement would lead to the replacement of powerful conservative Democrats in Congress and bring fundamental changes to the entire United States. SNCC workers often devoted months, if not years, to the communities in which they worked. When Dr. King came to town, thousands followed him and his magic name into the streets. But when he went home, many who had followed him also went home, and the movement came to a halt in its tracks. SNCC wanted a permanent commitment to struggle and change. By defining the struggle in terms of changing individuals, SNCC was setting up a revolution that it had an excellent chance of achieving. In the South, fear had for generations kept black people from their rights. By proving their willingness to march downtown in the face of police threats and arrests, and by having the courage to register to vote even, every person in the ranks of the movement had already achieved a revolution.

The next day someone from SNCC showed up and got me out of jail. But my days in town were numbered. A few days later as I passed by the town hall, which housed the city jail, I couldn't resist stopping to make a picture of the building with a few policemen peering out through the glass doors. It was a mistake. Soon I was back inside the jail, surrounded by Albany police. "Who are you anyway?" a detective asked as they pressed around me. My hands were trembling. I was terrified. "You're shaking now boy," he said. "You're going to be shaking a lot harder when we're done with you."

I left town the next day. Heading north to show my pictures, going back for my last year of college.

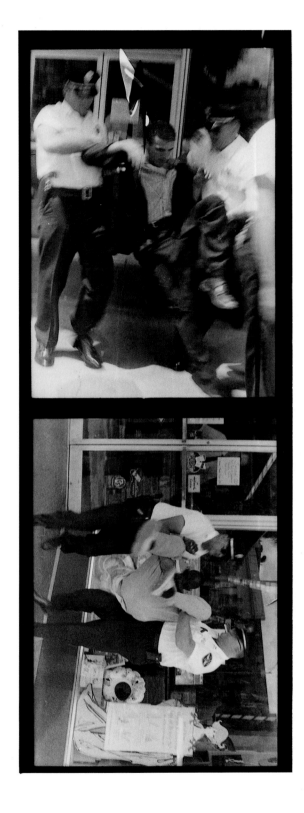

The first sit-in arrests I see and photograph are those of Eddie Brown, a former Albany gang leader, and a visitor from the North. Both have volunteered to be arrested for the photographs. The picture of Eddie Brown, calmly being carried off by the Albany police, is widely distributed as the image of the classic non-violent arrest.

Mississippi
September 1962

My final year at the University of Chicago was divided between being a student and making trips back to the South. I met Paul Brooks, another one of the original Freedom Riders out of Nashville, although I don't recall that he or anyone else ever brought this up, saying only that he was "from SNCC." SNCC and the Friends of SNCC in Chicago were using my photographs from Cairo and Albany. Harry Belafonte had been a staunch financial backer of SNCC all along. Brooks went to Belafonte and asked for $300, with which I was to buy a ticket to Jackson, Mississippi, where I would make pictures of Bob Moses.

When the DC-8 landed in Jackson, I might as well have been stepping off in Johannesburg. Everything frightened me. I was supposed to take a colored cab into a colored neighborhood, but it was illegal for black drivers to carry white passengers. And, needless to say, I couldn't ask a white driver to take me to look for civil rights workers. Eventually I persuaded some brave black driver to take me to the address I had been given for the Freedom House, the occupants of which told me I was at the wrong address. The Freedom House was next door. At the correct house, I was told I would find Mr. Moses at Amzie Moore's house up north in Cleveland in the Mississippi Delta. Passing the segregation signs that, though illegal, were still standing in front of the bus terminal, I rode up the highways to the rich, flat land created by the wanderings of the Mississippi in the northwest corner of the state below Memphis, where single-lane highways run on raised roadbeds through miles of unfenced fields.

From the window of my Greyhound bus

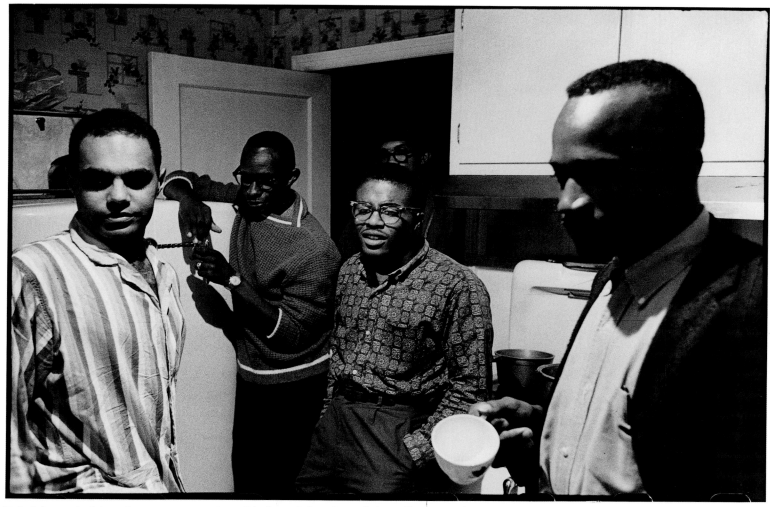

Bob Moses, in his pajamas, next to Sam Block and (on the right) Willie Peacock at Amzie Moore's house in Cleveland, Mississippi

In a Ruleville Freedom House, I, in deep cover, and Frank Smith take turns posing before a door perforated by the shotguns of night riders

It was September, and tufts of cotton that had fallen from wagons lay along the highway. Afraid to ask directions, I walked through Cleveland looking for the address I had been given in Jackson. Finally I stood before a small frame house and knocked on the door. A woman looked at the address I had written down. "This is *North* Magnolia. You want *South* Magnolia. That's over in niggertown." It was sunny and hot as I turned and walked all the way back to the center of town and then out toward the other side. For someone trying to slip quietly into town, I wasn't doing a very good job. I was more than relieved when the screen door opened and I stepped inside the house of Amzie Moore. Mr. Moore, a local NAACP leader, had been in the movement before there was one. He had been helping Bob Moses for two years.

I was probably as strange a sight to the people at Amzie Moore's house as they were to me. Since June, SNCC had set up its first five voter registration workers in the Delta—all male, all black. Moses came out in his pajamas to see me. Eventually I ended up in nearby Ruleville, where Frank Smith showed me a door full of shotgun holes. Night riders had been shooting into the house. Frank Smith and I took turns with my camera taking pictures of each other in front of the door. In the morning we went out to look at the plantations, and at night we drove to a church way back in the woods for a voter registration meeting. I remember how dark it was and how few people came to learn how to fill out the forms. At the time virtually no blacks were registered in the Mississippi Delta. And those few brave ones that tried could lose their homes, as did Fannie Lou Hamer, lose their jobs when their names were published in the newspaper, or lose their lives like Herbert Lee, who had been murdered for registering the year before in Liberty, Mississippi.

Mr. Amzie Moore
614 Chrisman Avenue
Cleveland, Mississippi

Dear Mr. Moore:

The Student Nonviolent Coordinating Committee, established at Raleigh, N. C. on April 17, 1960, is composed of students leaders from the thirteen Southern states and the District of Columbia. We serve as the coordinating body for the student movement.

For some time, we have been trying to improve the system of communication among students, especially in the deep South. This is vital to the movement. We n ow have a student who is traveling into Alabama, Louisiana, and Mississippi for the express purpose of meeting students and active adults in order to better our communication.

Mr. Robert Moses has worked closely with the Southern Christian Leadership Conference and with our Committee this summer. He left Atlanta on August 13 to go into the three states mentioned above. He will be in Mississippi during the week of August 17 to 25th approximately.

★ ★ ★

Sincerely yours,

Jane Stembridge

This letter was the first communication between the new student movement and Amzie Moore. Moore told Moses that, rather than trying to recruit students in Mississippi, it would be better to bring student activists into the state to spark a movement there.

When I asked Charlie Cobb if I could get away with photographing them while they canvassed in Ruleville, he said, "Probably, the first time." So we did it. Once. I was less lucky when I returned to Cleveland. While I was taking pictures in the street near Amzie Moore's house, a squad car pulled up next to me and the policeman inside told me to get in. Taken down to what looked like a small town hall, I was asked what I was doing, and when I answered that I was taking pictures, I was told I had to post a $1,000 bond "to be engaged in the business of photography" in Cleveland, Mississippi. I said I wasn't in business, so the city official, who was quite polite, showed me the statute in the book. He was firm. If I wanted to take photographs, I had to post a bond. Almost as if it were a joke, I asked if he would take a check. Then I said I'd return with the money and left. Outside in the parking lot, the officer who had picked me up was waiting. He was armed and he was very upset. "You can't go back and forth to niggertown. We don't do that down here. You stay in the white town or you stay with the niggers. We don't mix the races down here." Races in the South, as everywhere else in the world, were, in fact, very mixed up. Blacks grew up in the white world and passed as whites. White children were raised in the black world and were considered colored. I didn't want to be excluded from Amzie Moore's house and the movement. So I said I was colored. Only I made a serious error. "As a matter of fact, my grandfather was colored," I said. I was supposed to have said my grand*mother* was colored, and the policeman went nuts. "I'm going to blow your fuckin' brains out." He was livid. "If I see you anywhere I'm going to kill you."

It was a long walk back to Amzie's house. I kept hoping someone would pass in a car and get me out of there. I think finally someone did stop and take me to Amzie's. At seven the next morning I was standing by the highway waiting for a bus north to Oxford, Mississippi, home of William Faulkner and Ole Miss. James Meredith, an army veteran, was about to become the first black to enroll at the University of Mississippi. It would take an army of U.S. marshalls and two deaths—one of a journalist from France—to get him into his dorm.

That fall I was back riding my repaired motorcycle around the campus of the University of Chicago. One day I ran into Dona Richards, a very close friend who was a black New Yorker and a fellow student at the university. Excitedly, I told her of what I had seen. "Dona, there's a revolution going on in Mississippi." "Bullshit," she answered, "that's impossible." For most people in the North in 1962, black or white, what I had seen in Mississippi was impossible. *No one* believed that the southern blacks in Mississippi would rise up and fight for their rights. The press certainly did not believe it. As far as the media was concerned, aside from the drama of a bus getting bombed or a riot at Ole Miss, the civil rights movement that students had been carrying on for two-and-a-half years did not exist. In November Dona went to the SNCC conference in Nashville. In 1963 she went south to join the staff and went to work in Mississippi, and for awhile she and Bob Moses were married.

Bob Moses appears to us as an enigmatic leader of SNCC partly because he chose to appear that way. He was the rare example of a leader who refuses leadership. He genuinely believed that leadership should emerge from the community, and indeed the movement saw countless examples of this. Although later on in the decade all kinds of leaders, real and assumed, would revel in the glare of publicity, during the movement it was very un-SNCC-like to put yourself in the limelight. However enamored I was of Lewis and Forman, at age twenty I did not want to be led. I wanted to lead myself. So did everyone.

(*Above and right*) *Children work in the cotton fields.*
(*Below*) *Voter registration workers, including Charlie Cobb, Charles MacLaurin, and Jesse Harris, in a rural Delta church*

Frank Smith, Bob Moses, and Willie Peacock in the Greenwood SNCC office in March 1963. The office is firebombed the next day.

In 1962 Bob Moses requested conscientious objector status from the Selective Service. On the following pages are selections from a rather good biography prepared by an anonymous government investigator. Moses did not receive CO status and later, in the 1960s, he fled to Canada and then settled with his family in Africa rather than serve in the armed forces in Vietnam.

U. S. ATTORNEY

1962 MAR 23 PM 3:33

Resume of the Inquiry

Re: Robert Parris Moses

Conscientious Objector

Registrant was born in New York City on January 23, 1935. His parents were members of the Baptist Church and the registrant formerly attended that church but claims membership in no religious organization.

The records of Stuyvesant High School in New York City show that the registrant attended there from September 1945 until his graduation in June 1952 and was rated 320 in a class of 750; that only a select group of students are taken at that high school and that he rated as very intelligent with outstanding personality and character; that he was president of his senior class and also received a scholarship award. A teacher in this school recalled the registrant as being quiet, reserved, soft spoken and a good athlete. He could not comment on the registrant's claim. The records of Hamilton College, Clinton, New York show that the registrant attended there from September 1952 until his graduation in June 1956 with an A. B. degree and attaining an 85 percent average; that he majored in philosophy and had been active in baseball and basketball, was a member of the Honor Court in his junior year and was basketball captain and class vice president in his senior year; that he was granted a $900 scholarship and given opportunity to earn $200 additional by employment in the Commons. An official of this college recalled the registrant as a fine student, reputable, capable and conscientious; that he knew nothing of registrant's feeling toward military service but he would not be surprised if the registrant held conscientious-objector beliefs because of his

quiet manner; that he had read of the registrant's
activity with the Freedom Riders in the south.   An
instructor in this school advised that he considered
the registrant to be a reputable, capable and loyal
American; that he did not have any indication that the
registrant either favored or opposed military service;
that he believed him sincere and honest and therefore
probably possessed of the convictions on military service
he claimed to have.   The records of Harvard University,
Cambridge, Massachusetts show that the registrant was
awarded a Masters of Arts degree in June 1957 by the
Harvard Graduate School of Arts and Sciences; that he
majored in philosophy at Harvard from September 1956 to
March 1958 when he withdrew with a B average; that his
records were incomplete and he failed a preliminary
examination for a Doctor of Philosophy degree in May
1957.   An instructor in this university who is a member
of the Society of Friends advised that he knew the
registrant to be interested in the philosophy of pacifism
and nonviolence and he believed the registrant would
be sincere in his conscientious objection.

* * *

A
representative of Horace Mann School advised that the
registrant had taught mathematics at that school during
the school years from 1958 to 1961 and was an excellent
teacher; that he resigned to go south and help his
race get registered so that they could vote and that he
had been arrested in Mississippi in October 1961.   She
believed he would be sincere in his claim.

* * *

A representative of the Student Nonviolent
Coordinating Committee (SNCC), Atlanta, Georgia advised
that he has known the registrant since July 1961 and that
he is of good character, sincere in his beliefs and
considered a genius by his associates; that he abhors
violence and his work with the SNCC is an example of
the extent to which he will go to avoid violence; that
he has been beaten three times during demonstrations
in Mississippi and while being beaten will look up and
say "Forgive them"; that the registrant has never discussed
conscientious objection with him but he believed registrant to be conscientiously opposed to service in the
Armed Forces; that the registrant has donated his time
to the organization and his only compensation has been
room and board; that the SNCC does not have a charter
and the by-laws of the organization have not been written
but the purpose was stated at their Raleigh conference
as assuming a philosophical or religious ideal of nonviolence from Judaic-Christian traditions seeking a
social order of justice, permeated by love.   Another
representative of this organization advised that the
registrant has been associated with that committee since
July 1961; that he came to Atlanta in the summer of 1960
to aid the Negro race and had a Masters degree in philosophy;

The registrant's father advised that he has three sons and that when his wife died in 1958 he had a nervous breakdown, went to a hospital and the family broke up; that the registrant went to stay with an aunt; that the registrant is of good character, intelligent, a deep thinker and sincere in everything he does; that religion was not pushed at him and he went only occasionally to Sunday School at St. Mark's Church at 133th Street and St. Nicholas Avenue in New York City and he did not know of any church of which the registrant was a member; that at one time while attending Hamilton College the registrant had written that he was sincere about becoming a minister and that he had told his son that the ministry was a calling, not just an occupation; that the registrant had told him during his junior or senior year at Hamilton College that he was going to file a conscientious-objector claim; that he had told the registrant "All Hell would break out" and that the registrant had said that the worst that could happen to him would be that he would spend a few years in jail; that he himself has worked at an Armory for a number of years and that one son has spent two years in the Army and another son is presently in the Army in Europe. He was sure that the registrant is sincere in his conscientious-objector claim.

★ ★ ★

Credit records were negative. Records of the Pike County Jail, Magnolia, Mississippi show that the registrant was admitted to the jail on October 31, 1961 and was released on $1,000 bail on December 6, 1961. The records of McComb, Mississippi Police Department show that the registrant was charged on October 4, 1961 with disturbing the peace and was found guilty before a Justice of the Peace on October 31, 1961; that an affidavit in the files filed by a police officer charged the registrant with contributing to the delinquency of a minor 16 years of age by encouraging the child to violate the laws of Mississippi. A Justice of the Peace at McComb advised that the registrant was brought into his court on August 15, 1961 charged with interfering with a policeman in the performance of his duty and that he had found the registrant guilty and fined him $50 with $5 costs and offered to suspend the $50 fine if the registrant would not return to court for 90 days; that the registrant refused to pay the $5 cost and was then remanded to the Pike County Jail; that a Negro attorney then came and paid the registrant's way out of jail for $49 representing the $50 fine and $5 cost less the two days in jail at $3 a day. He advised that the attorney had indicated at the time that he intended to appeal the conviction.

Prepared: March 21, 1962

Nashville, November 1962
The Annual SNCC Conference

The annual SNCC conference brings together the field staff and supporters from the North. Virtually everyone attending this conference is marching downtown to demonstrate.

The fall 1962 SNCC conference was held in Nashville. Fieldworkers who came from across the South mixed with Nashville students and northerners like me; as part of the conference, everyone formed orderly lines and, led by movement veterans, marched into downtown Nashville. Many segregated stores simply locked the doors to keep us out. As we stood outside a Tic Toc hamburger place, employees would let in a local white, then slam the door on the waiting line of demonstrators. Sam Block, the field secretary from Greenwood, led the line I was watching. As he stood near the partly open door, an arm reached out and stabbed Sam in the chest with a pen. He staggered back in pain and, not wanting to show the crowd what had happened, bravely led the line away as Peg Dammond and Lester MacKinney tried to help him.

That night SNCC held a rally in a church basement. One of the pictures on my contact sheet shows chairman McDew and secretary Forman counting up the nickels, dimes, and quarters from the collection.

Chuck McDew's initial reaction to the movement in 1960 had been to try to stay out of it, an understandable decision considering that, as he drove from Ohio through the South to the first SNCC conference, he was stopped by a policeman, and when he refused to say "yes sir," the policeman broke his jaw. "These people are crazy," McDew later recalled. "I'm getting out." But he didn't get out; he stayed.

He became the first SNCC chairman and joined Moses in jail in McComb. A converted Jew, McDew liked to quote from rabbinical writings to explain his actions: "If I am not for myself, who will be for me? If I am for myself only, what am I? If not now, when?"

McDew and I became good friends, and that winter we did some fund raising at Lucy Montgomery's house in Chicago. Lucy, a white southerner, was one of SNCC's most faithful supporters. Things must have gotten out of hand, because the last thing I recall after talking to her parrot was having to run out of the house with Chuck, who drove while I vomited onto the side of my car, where it froze. I guess I wasn't very good at fund raising.

Chuck McDew, Joni Rabinowitz, and Jack Chatfield locked out of a downtown department store

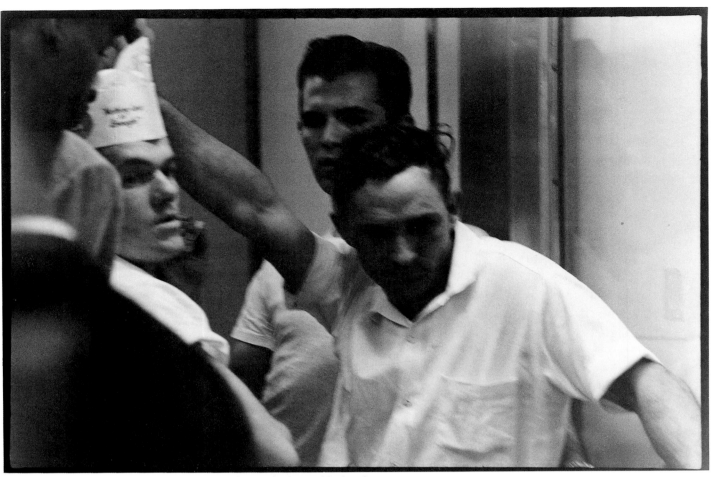

At a Nashville Tic Toc restaurant, a defiant employee blocks the entrance.

Outside, Lester MacKinney, Bernice Reagon, and John O'Neal wait to get in.

Joy Reagon   *Jessie Harris*   *Peggy Dammond   Sam Block*   *Dorie Ladner*

Trying to enter the Tic Toc, Sam Block is stabbed in the chest with a pen. In pain, he is led away.

Jack Chatfield   *John O'Neal*   *Sam Block*

Chairman Chuck McDew speaking at the Nashville conference

The meeting ends, as does virtually every movement meeting, with the singing of "We Shall Overcome."

Cordell and Bernice Reagon and Willie Peacock, three of the original Freedom Singers, lead an audience that includes McDew and Forman, June Johnson, Bob Zellner, McArthur Cotton, Avon Rollins, Ben Grinidge, Joy Reagon, Hollis Watkins, and Porter Davis.

In February 1963, Jimmy Travis, a twenty-year-old Mississippi native, will survive an assassination attempt on Bob Moses as they drive together outside of Greenwood. Travis is hit in the neck and shoulder.

53

Mississippi, 1963

Many in the movement believe an organized effort is underway to depopulate black areas of the South.

Greenwood, Mississippi   March 27, 1963

Last night two shotgun blasts were fired into the home of Mr.
Dewey Green, Sr. in Greenwood, Mississippi. Mr. Green's sons have
both been active in the struggle for civil rights in the South.
One applied for admission at the University of Mississippi; the other
isxactive in the Missipsippi voter registration project.

This morning, in what is an obvious answer to white Mississippi's
violence, 120 Negro prospective voter applicants gathered in front of
Weslian Methodist Church in Greenwood to march on the courthouse and
attempt to register to vote.

On March 24th Greenwood, Mississippi became the scene of violence
for the fifth time since February 20th. The office of the Student
Nonviolent Coordinating Committee and a cleaning and pressing establishment xxxx 1,500 feet east of the office were gutted by fire.
Samuel Block, SNCC Field Secretary in Leflore County, says the police
were contacted shortly after the fires were started at 12:00 a.m. but
that the police didn't arrive until ten in the morning. The fire
destroyed a $800 mimeograph machine, two typewriters and important
records.

On February 20th four small businesses, located on the same
block as the Greenwood office of SNCC, were destroyed by fire. Samuel
Block was arrested for stating that the arson was an attempt to burn
down the SNCC office. He was found guilty of "issuing statements
calculated to breach the peace" and sentenced to six months in jail
and fined $500.

On Thursday evening, February 28th, James Travis, a 20 year old
SNCC staff member, was shot in the neck and shoulder when the car
which he was driving was shot into by three white men, seven miles
outside of Greenwood.

Four voter registration workers were cut by flying glass when
the car in which they were sitting was fired into on Wednesday
night, March 7th.

The Student Nonviolent Coordinating Committee requested the
Federal Government to use its Executive or Judicial arms to protect
the citizens of Greenwood, Mississippi. The Student Nonviolent
Coordinating Committee is asking for Federal Troops and Federal
Marshalls to protect Greenwood citizens,

Today 100 persons marched in the courthouse in Greenwood. The
police set dogs on the people and ten to twelve were arrested, including James Foreman. The police then entered the church headquarters of the group and arrested more persons. The police are
standing in front of the courthouse with guns. A mob of whites is
forming.

One of the early press releases from the Greenwood SNCC office

Winona, Mississippi
June 9, 1963

Euvester Simpson

Annell Ponder

June Johnson

Annel Ponder describing events in Winona, Miss. to Jean Levine, Wiley Branton's secretary.

Miss Levine: Describe what happened to you from the time you went into the bus station.

Ponder: Well, this is what happened. We left there, at Winona, at about 11:15 Sunday morning and then 3 or 4 of us got off the bus and went into the cafe to be served, and we sat down at the lunch counter and when we sat down there were 2 waitresses back of the counter and one of them just balled up her dish cloth, the wash cloth she had in her hand and threw it against the wall behind us. She said, "I can't take no more", and so right after she said that the chief of police and highway patrolman came from the rear area of the cafe and came around and tapped us on the shoulder with the billy clubs. Said "y'all get out, get out". We all stood up when he tapped us and when he got to me I said, "you know, it's against the law to put us out of here", don't you". He said, "ain't no damn law, you just get out of here". So we went on the outside and stood and talked about this for about 5 to 8 minutes and 2 other people, Euvesta Simpson and Rosemary Freeman joined us out there. As I understand it, they had been in the restaurant. Euvesta had tried to go to the rest room and one of the policeman had told her to go to a segregated one. He pointed out which one for her to go to, and so she came out and was telling us about that and we stood around talking a few minutes. I went back to the door and looked in to get a better look at the patrolmen, the officers. They saw us looking in and then we came back out and stood and talked some more. We were just discussing it, what happened, and I said, well, we ought to get something and make a report on this, so then I happened to think the patrol car was right out there. So I said we could get the license plate number of the patrol car and we went around to the back to get this and as I was writing it down the patrolman and the chief of police came out of the restaurant. The chief of police said, "You're all under arrest", you're under arrest. Get in that car there." They had us get into the patrolman's car. As we were getting in the car Mrs. Hamer got off the bus and

In a notorious incident, four movement women, Fannie Lou Hamer, Annell Ponder of the SCLC, Euvester Simpson, and sixteen-year-old June Johnson, were arrested in Winona, Mississippi, as they returned from a workshop at the Highlander Center. Three of them were beaten in the jail. When Lawrence Guyot went to try to bond them out, he, too, was badly beaten. Above and following is an account given by Annell Ponder and Fannie Lou Hamer a few days afterward.

asked us if we wanted them to go on down to Greenwood. So I said yes, and then
the chief of police hollared out, "get that one there, get that one there, bring
her on down in the other car". So he got Mrs. Hamer and brought her on down -
took us all down to the jail and when we got down there he didn't say what he
charged us with. He said "you'all are raising hell all over the place". And
then they took us inside and had us standing up and starting asking some questions
Then they separated us, put some of us in the cell, and never did say what they
were locking us up for. All of us were put in a cell except June Johnson; she
was the last one out so they started talking to her and asking her questions and
I understand one of them saying something like, "Well, what do you think we're
supposed to do about that?." One of the officers said, "Well, what do you think
we're supposed to do about that?" And I could hear her say, "you all are suppps-
ed to protect us and take care of us," And after that I heard her screaming and
we could hear sounds of blows. They beat her a few minutes and then they came
and got me out and sent her where I was and I passed her on the way out and she
was bleeding in the face and she was crying. There was blood on the floor of
the room where she had been and they told me to stand over there where she had
been. So I went over and stood where she had been and they stood around about
½ a minute and then they started in asking me questions, started hitting me. One
said to me "you all are down there stirring up shit and the more we stir the more
it stank, you all were doing a demonstration".. We were not, we had not planned
a demonstration at all, we just went in there to eat, so we tried to explain this
and they kept wanting me to say yes sir, "I want to hear you say, yes sir, nigger
Before they had separated us up in the cells, one officer in a blue uniform
wanted to know if I had enough respect for him to say yes sir, and I told him
I didn' know him that well. So as he looked at me with a kind of amazed look,
then after that they just kept trying to get me to say yes sir, and I wouldn't
and they kept hitting me, from one to the other and around, and this went on for

about 10 minutes, talking and beating. I'd say there were at least 3, the highway patrolman, the blue-uniformed officer (I guess a local policeman), then ther
was a man who did not have on a uniform, but he was a short man, but we saw him,
he was there yesterday when we got out. I could identify him easily. One fello
Squeaky, from down in Greenwood, has some good pictures we can use to identify
them later on. Anyway, at least 3 of them kind of gave us the run over with
black jacks, a belt, fists, open palm and at one point the highway patrolman hit
me in the stomach. That went on off and on I guess about 10 minutes, talking an
beating - they really wanted to make me say yes sir and that's one thing that I
wouldn't say. After they got through beating me they took a white fellow out of
the cell and put him in a cell with some more white men and put me in the cell
he was in because the other cells were full - there were 2 to each cell. I was
in a cell by myself. By this time it was Sunday afternoon. They brought us
something to eat. A man kept saying "you, black, African-looking son-of-a-bitch
This is what they kept calling me. Even after I had passed the room the man in
the blue uniform would look in and yell that out. He kept insisting that I call
him Mr. So I asked him at one point why was it so important and then he'd just
get angry again and start hitting me again. We were in jail until about 4:30

★   ★   ★

Jack Minnis asks Fannie Lou Hamer to give her account of what happened.
This excerpt begins with Miss Hamer listening to Annell Ponder being beaten.

★   ★   ★

You know, that
screaming and all of that will always follow me - I never will forget it and they
whipped her, and after awhile she passed by where we was in the cell and her
mouth was bleeding and her hair was standing up on her head and it was horrifying.
So then after they decided to stop, well, this man asked me where was I from -
the state highway patrolman - he asked me where was I from and I told him I was
from Ruleville, so he said, well I'm going to check and see. And I figured well
it wasn't going to be nothing happen to me because, I told him, I say, after all,
I was born, I think it was, in this county, Montgomery County. He said, "and you
stay in Ruleville now?" I say, yes sir. So he said, "well, I'm going to check,

I'm going to see where you're from." So I know ~~byxymxkmmwixg~~, you know, by me being one of the persons that works with this voter registration when he checked well that really was going to put me on the spot. So when he walked back in there he said, "yes, you live in Ruleville" and said "you the big..." and I've never heard that many names called a human in my life. He used all kinds of curse words. So one of the officers called me fatso, and then he said, "let's take her in here". So they carried me in a room and it was 2 Negro boys in this room. So the state highway patrol gave them a long blackjack and it was wide and he told one of the boys, said "take this". And he said, "this what you want me to use?" He said, "that's right" and said, "if you don't use it on her, you know what I'll use on you". So then the boy told me "get over there". I say, "where?". And he said, "on that cot". I said, "you mean you would do this to your own race?" Then this state patrolman said "you heard what I told you". He say, "all right/, get over there and stretch out". So then I had to get over there on the bed, ~~apside~~ of my stomach and that man beat me, that man beat me ti]

and
~~ixgixx~~ he give out,/by me screaming, made one of the other ones, a plain clothes
fellow   on
~~xmm~~, he didn't have/~~nmxamtfmrm~~ nothing like a uniform, he got so hot and worked up off it, he just come there, you know, and start hitting on the back of my head. Well, my hands, I was trying to guard some of the licks, you see, my hands they just beat my hands til they turned blue. And after he had finished, well my clothes, quite naturally, you know, beating me like that, my clothes come up and I tried to pull them down, you know, it was just pitiful. And then, one of the white fellows, one of the other white fellows, just take my clothes and snatched them up and this Negro when he had beat me til he was just, I know he was give out, well then this state patrolman told the other Negro to beat me, so he taken over from there. And he just beat til, and anywhere you could see me you could see I'm not lying, because, you know, I just can sit down, I've been sleeping on my faith and I was just as hard as a bone.

One of the SNCC posters printed by Mark Suckle from a photograph I made on the University of Mississippi campus when James Meredith tried to register as the first black student there

Danville, Virginia
June 10, 1963

The cover of the Danville pamphlet written by Dottie Miller and printed in August 1963 in Atlanta by SNCC's communications department, run by Julian Bond. It used my photographs and layout along with lists of the people injured to document the police attacks and publicize the Danville movement.

Back in Chicago, I was finally done with my college courses. It had been a hard wait. In May demonstrations had broken out in Birmingham, and the films and photographs of high school students being knocked around with high-pressure water hoses proved irresistible to the press. Two-and-a-half years after it had begun in earnest, the civil rights movement was finally discovered by the American media. It was a front-page story and would remain so until displaced by Vietnam.

The same front page of the May 2 *New York Times* that ran photographs of Birmingham also ran a story about an integrated group of five CORE workers and four

SNCC workers who were arrested as they tried to walk into Alabama in a continuation of William Moore's march. Moore, a white postman and CORE member from Baltimore, had been murdered a few weeks earlier as he walked through the South carrying a sign saying, "Eat at Joe's, Both Black and White." The leader of what was called the "Postman's March" was a twenty-year-old white Alabaman named Sam Shirah. When arrested, all the marchers were taken to Kilby State Prison, where they refused bond and proceeded to go on a hunger strike. Eric Weinberger of CORE was still not eating after seventeen days.

On June 10, the day after the beatings in the Winona jail, I finally flew from Chicago to Atlanta to take the job that Forman had offered me as staff photographer for SNCC. At the Atlanta airport I had boarded a bus and was sitting in the back waiting to go downtown when someone started pounding on the window. It was Forman. He told me to get off the bus. "Got any money on you?" he asked—an almost traditional way to greet a northerner. "Then go to the Delta ticket counter and buy a ticket to Danville." I took the suitcase I had brought from Chicago to Atlanta and went up to Delta. "I'd like a ticket to Danville," I said. "Where's Danville?" Since no other seats were available, I flew first class with Forman and Leo Brandon, an attorney from Los Angeles.

Danville is a textile town in southern Virginia that is dominated by the huge textile manufacturer, Dan River Mills. That day, June 10, 1963, had been one of the most brutal in the history of the movement, and the gruesome reports were still coming in to the Atlanta office. In the afternoon, police using clubs and fire hoses had attacked demonstrators who were praying at city hall, sending most to the hospital. When we reached Danville, Jim Forman and I picked up Dottie Miller, who had been clubbed, and we drove straight to Winslow Hospital, the Negro hospital. Although there were three doctors in my immediate family, I didn't even know there *were* such things as Negro hospitals. Wounded people were sitting on the floor in the halls. People with lacerations and fractures were lying on stretchers waiting to be stitched up. Forman kept telling me to take close-ups of the wounds. Later I photographed a man whose shirt front was completely covered with his own dried blood. His broken arm was in a sling. Next to him stood his friend, one eye swollen and closed, his head split open in two places; sutured closed, the swelling rose about two inches above his scalp. These people had been kneeling and praying at the city hall.

The Danville police attack that day had been so brutal that forty-eight out of sixty-five demonstrators were injured. Dottie Miller's head was lacerated and her sandals knocked off by the hoses. Dottie, who had been with SNCC for eighteen months and usually worked in the office, where she and Julian Bond ran the communications department, was the first to call the report in to Atlanta. When eighteen-year-old Bob Mants picked up the phone, she just broke down and cried. Later Dottie told me, "You were supposed to be so brave you weren't supposed to cry."

A few days later a couple of hundred demonstrators returned to city hall, occupying the front steps. As darkness fell some left, but the remainder vowed to stay all night. The tension mounted. Police again marched down to the city hall, brandishing nightsticks. Unwound coils of high-pressure fire hoses lay crisscrossing the pavement in the light of street lamps. Up on the steps with the demonstrators sat Dottie Miller, clutching a railing with all her might. "We were getting ready to be killed." Just at that moment, Forman jumped up from among the demonstrators and walked straight at the police. "Now wait a minute. What's going on here?" he shouted. When the firemen and police hesitated, the demonstrators vacated the steps. Dottie Miller never forgot Forman at that moment. "He saved our lives."

Dottie Miller, who lost her shoes to high-pressure fire hoses after being clubbed, gives an affidavit to James Forman.

A crowd watches the demonstrators returning to the city hall steps.

Some of the wounded demonstrators in the High Street Baptist Church

Ivanhoe Donaldson, Marion Barry, and James Forman

Bob Zellner, Bernice Reagon, Cordell Reagon, Dottie Miller (Zellner), and Avon Rollins

Outside a packed Danville mass meeting, the crowd responds to speeches and singing by SNCC workers.

On the final evening I was in Danville, a mass meeting was held in a cinderblock church at the edge of town. During the meeting, word came that police and a tank—of all things—were waiting up the road. The meeting, which was crowded with children, broke up. The SNCC staff, divided by sex and packed into two cars, were the very last to leave. Forman was there, along with Marion Barry, Ivanhoe Donaldson, Dottie Miller, and Bob Zellner, whom Dottie would soon marry. I was torn between the thrill of being squashed in a car with so many of the movement leaders and fear of the tank silhouetted up ahead. The police, having beaten up so many demonstrators, had now turned to the state national guard for more powerful weapons. They had also buried the entrance to the police station in sandbags. The more violence they committed, the more violence they seemed to expect.

I had also been playing a role as a spy of sorts. Forman had asked me to go through the files at the local newspaper office to try to find more photographs of the brutality. The local photographer I had conned my way into a relationship with was now standing with the heavily armed police as they stopped the first car and told us to get out. The entire staff were standing in the night, spread-eagled against the cars as men holding shotguns patted us down. I had some film jammed into my pocket, and the policeman felt it as he ran his hands up and down my legs. I kept thinking of Camus's description of the execution of French resistance workers, who were told to run into a field, where the Nazis shot them. "What's this?" asked the trooper. "It's my film," I said. Just then the reporter I had befriended with stories about how people in Chicago "really admire how you handle the niggers down here" came up to us, Speed Graflex in hand. He was using a flash to make pictures of everyone. Apparently shocked to see me in such company, he stepped back and said, "And you're a liar, too," and he took my picture spread-eagled next to Forman. After the shakedown, they finally let the two carloads of SNCC people pass. That night arrest warrants were issued for twenty-two SNCC workers under a state law originally passed after Nat Turner's rebellion and used to hang John Brown: "Inciting the colored population to acts of war and violence against the white population." I believe at that time the crime was punishable by death.

After the mass meeting broke up, the SNCC leadership became virtual prisoners in the High Street Baptist Church, which was a sanctuary against arrest. (Eventually police broke the door down and arrested everyone anyway.) Forman told Dottie and me to leave and return to the Atlanta office, as there was really no point in our being arrested. We left the next morning by climbing out a back window of the church, then going down through the woods to a small American Legion hall. I kept looking at a case full of rifles as we waited there for the woman in whose house we had slept to arrive in her large pink Cadillac. We got behind the seats and covered ourselves with newspaper—a pointless tactic apparently, because when we reached the airport it was swarming with reporters waiting, I assumed, to film our arrest. I walked past the news crews and asked for the tickets I had reserved for Paul Newman and Joanne Woodward. The newsmen, who must have been waiting for someone more important to arrive, ignored us.

That evening, about ten days after my graduation, I finally reached Atlanta. It was the middle of a period that historian Taylor Branch calls "the Firestorm." From May to September, fourteen thousand people were arrested in communities across the South. The movement had reached its zenith.

The mass meeting in Danville is so crowded that it overflows out into the yard. When word arrives that heavily armed police and an armored vehicle are waiting up the road, the crowd disperses, leaving the SNCC workers to exit last.

James Forman, like many of the SNCC field staff, was a powerful stump speaker. Here he works the crowd at the Danville mass meeting. An hour later he will be searched by police holding shotguns and automatic weapons.

Gadsden, Alabama
June 1963

In addition to my Nikon, I traveled with a small, portable Olivetti typewriter. At Gadsden I typed out a conversation I had carried on with members of the Alabama Highway Patrol as I made pictures of them.

```
        Gadsden, Alabama          June 27, 1963

A Conversation with the Alabama Highway Patrol

(Five squad cars were parked on the highway observing
the activities acrossthe street at the Skyliner Motel.
Demonstrators wandered in and out of the building
preparing for the days activities. I wandered across
the street, introduced myself as a photographer working
for a quasi-fascist news agency in Chicago, and spent
the next few hours in quasi-fascist conversation with
the police. They were friendly; one suggested that in
two months I'd not want to leave the South. Passing the
day with them would convert me, he said. The following
comments were made by the officers;)

----They're getting four dollars a day, each. In Birm-
ingham some of them got $17.50 a day. We know they
get paid; too many ofthem said it for it not to be true.

----(The police spoke a great deal about what we would
call police brutality. Themore intellegent ones, or honest
might be better, seemed troubled and  offered elaborate
explanations: Prod poles were more humane than sticks.
A local citizen put it this way -- they hurt but do
not harm. Another mentionedthat it was also for the
Negro demonstrators that five cops were used for each.
A larger force could less painfully subdue a demonstrator.
One cop knew of the North)  In Chicago they're really
tough. I was told they just pick a coloredfellow off
the street a beathis head in...Did you see Wallace on
television in New York? He had all th statistics. The
amount of people hurt in Birmingham was much less than
in any raceriot of the North.
                                        KNOW
----(We spoke of mutual friends) You Forman? Is he up in
Danville? (Forman, I ask?) Yeah, F.O.R.M.A.N. He'sthe
field secretary from Atlanta; of CORE I think. I read
he is in jail in Danville. (Forman was at the time in
the meeting hall across the street.) Zellner is up there
too, another said.(It was kind of like name-dropping.

----(I noticed that an officer, sitting behind the wheel
of his car was going through a pile of 8/10 photos.)
That one's a Black Muslem I think. See,(pointing to
a black and white print of the front row in a Gadsden
Mass Meeting), red socks and red tie -- thats what they
```

wore in Birmingham. (He said a Birmingham news
man was sending them shots. Maybe I could send
shots of Danville leaders to check against those in
Gadsden?)

----(A rather heavy Negro boy, slovenly dressed and
blind in one eye was crossing the street about
50 feet from the squad cars. The sun was shinging
brightly, no demonstrators were to be seen, the police
were obviously getting bored) Lets get him over here -
I'd like to beat his head a little. Another called
the youth, who, turning in terror at the policemans
call, stood hesitatingly and looked two towards the
eight cops. Come-on boy, they insisted, andslowly,
with obvious fear the youth came and stood before the
police. The cop talked to him over th roof of a
squad car. (I couldn't hear the talk for one of the
men was speaking to me.) He's typical -- maybe a
bit above average. (General laughter) Is he the
leader, I asked? (No onelaughed) No. No, Hes not
the leader. (Eventually they lost interest and told the
boy to leave.)

----Three of the men had been busying themselves by
wrapping the length of their electric prod-poles in
black bape. I asked if I could take a shot, and
smiling the three posedwithere weapon. They make
alot of these in the North, they said? I explained
theat they were kind of exotic as tools of law enforcem
-ent. They assurred me that they only administer a
slight shock. In the background the three kept wrap-
ing black tape on the handles of their poles.

----The officer, somewhat more talkative than his men,
kept speaking of the eventsof Wenesday night. It
seemed to have bothered him. The police hurt no one
he insisted. Their sudden appearence from around the
side of the court house was enough to route the hundre
ds of demonstrators that lay on the court ho se lawn.
We didn't even tell them to go; they just saw us and
ran. (A minor tremor of pride passed through his men.)
You know what I'm convinced of, he said? Them kids
were fornicating on the court house lawn. He was sure
of it he said. They were lying there, it was three in
the morning. Three or four couples must have been fory

fornicating.
----Later they arrested 59 demonstrators for violating
     an injunction

Savannah, Georgia

In Savannah, hundreds of young people were going to jail in a movement led by Hosea Williams of the SCLC. Here, police arrest whites who are harassing demonstrators.

The office would just say, "Go to Savannah," and you'd go, hoping the address they gave you was correct—if they gave you an address. When I got there I didn't know anyone until I walked into the Freedom House, and there stood Casey, a friend from the Atlanta office.

Hosea Williams of the SCLC in Savannah

Marches in Savannah

Casey Hayden

Gadsden

Savannah

Arrests in Savannah

Demonstrators about to be arrested

The Leesburg, Georgia, Stockade

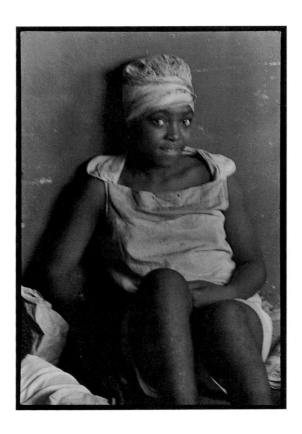

Arrested for demonstrating in Americus, Georgia, teenage girls are kept in a stockade in the countryside near Leesburg. They have no beds and no working sanitary facilities. I make pictures through the broken glass of the barred windows.

I am 13 years old and was in Leesburg stockade from August 31 to September 8. There were 32 kids in there with me. There were no beds, no mattresses, no blankets, pillows, no sheets. The floor was cold. You lay down for while and soon it starts hurting you so you sit up for awhile and it starts hurting so you have to walk around for a while.

The hamburgers were dry and were not cooked well because when you break your meat open you can see a lot of red meat inside.

The smell of the waste material was bad. I went to the bathroom there to urinate, but didn't have a bowel movement during the entire nine days I was there. I urinated where the water from the shower drains down. Some of the girls used a piece of cardboard that came from the boxes, the cardboard boxes, that the hamburgers were brought in.

The water was hot and it was running all the while. The man gave us three cups for the 32 of us.

There was a shower but it wasn't clean enough for you to bathe in. Cardboard with waste material had been put there and it needed cleaning and scrubbing.

At night the mosquitoes and roaches were at us. In the middle of the week the white man gave us some blankets. They were the ones which had been burned. He put them out in the sun and then gave them back to us. Two or three of us slept on one blanket.

Sworn before me this 13th day of September, 1963,

Lois Barnum Holley

Notary Public, Ga. State at large
My commission expires 8-29-67

Henrietta Fuller

Henrietta Fuller

In August reports of mass arrests came in to the office from Terrill County, but not much was known about them. So I was sent to Americus. The movement headquarters there was in a funeral home, I recall, and a young man offered to take me into the countryside, where a number of teenage girls were being held. Arrested during July and August for demonstrating in Americus, these girls had been transferred to the county stockade at Leesburg. My companion said he could distract the lone jailer, whom he called "Pops," giving me time to sneak around to the back and make photographs. When we got there I waited a moment for him to start talking to "Pops" before I crawled out of the back of the car and walked up to one of the windows of the stockade. Beautiful teenage girls came up to the window. They wanted to know my name and where I was from; it was a kind of surprise social event. We said things like "freedom," and they reached out to shake hands with me through the bars and broken glass of the window.

I couldn't make pictures with all of them crowded around, and I was worried about the jailer, so I asked a few girls to go up front and talk to him while I went around to make more pictures through the back window. The single toilet was clogged with feces. The only source of water was a dripping shower head. "Pops" apparently was feeding them on hamburgers he brought in once a day. Then the girls lay on the floor to show me how they slept. For all practical purposes the girls, many as young as thirteen and all rounded up after protest marches, had been forgotten by the world, including SNCC's Atlanta office, which had its hands full. I shook more hands, said "freedom" some more, and climbed back into the car, where I lay down in the well behind the seats. Unfortunately, my guide had never operated a manual-shift car, so we lurched off, bouncing up and down the road as we made our escape. That night I took my pictures back to Atlanta and processed them. Within days, SNCC had placed the pictures in the hands of a U.S. congressman, who entered them in the Congressional Record. Word quickly came back to Americus, and the girls, who were being held without charges, were released early in September.

Until that moment I don't think I had really been accepted into SNCC. After all, SNCC people were activists. Most of them went to jail routinely. They *did* things. It was one of their finest qualities. All I did was make pictures. But in Americus, my pictures had actually accomplished something. They had gotten people out of jail.

Back in Atlanta, I moved into an apartment with John Lewis, who had become chairman of SNCC, replacing Chuck McDew. (Twenty-eight years later, Congressman John Lewis still remembered the address of that apartment. Being hit over the head had not dulled his memory.) Our third roommate was Sam Shirah, whose father was a Methodist minister in Alabama and whose ancestors had fought for the Confederacy. Sam played the guitar, knew how charming he could be, and couldn't understand why the world had chosen Bob Dylan as its troubadour instead of him. Once he took me home to Troy, and we spent a night crawling up a hill where his ancestors had fought for the South. I think he wanted me to know just how southern he really was.

That a descendant of the Confederacy, a black Alabama farm boy, and a New York Jew were all living together said a great deal about what SNCC was like then. Eventually I brought south a 1956 black Oldsmobile and drove John to the office because he didn't know how to drive. I virtually became Jim Forman's chauffeur and did everything for him but wear a little cap. I would drive him somewhere and then jump out and run around to open the door, calling out "Mr. Forman" for everyone to hear. Once when he went north, Forman stayed with my parents at our home in Forest Hills, Queens, as many of the SNCC people did. His shoes were so worn that my mother managed to get him to leave wearing a pair of my father's. Then she kept Forman's old shoes and showed them to friends as a kind of holy relic.

The Atlanta office was on the second floor of a small, stuccoed building called the Marx Building, located on Raymond Street just off Auburn Avenue. Around the corner was Pasqual's, the best restaurant in black Atlanta. You could go to Pasqual's for breakfast, get a pork chop with eggs and grits, and eat it seated between Julian Bond, who was writing for SNCC, and Jeremiah X, who wrote for the widely read Muslim paper, *Mohammed Speaks*. Nearby was a small stand-up luncheonette with a jukebox crammed with the records of Joe Tex and James Brown.

Everything revolved around the office. You went there in the morning. You hung out there in the daytime. If you had a car and wanted to see a movie in the evening, you usually had twelve people who went with you and spent two hours discussing which movie to see. Eventually the office expanded to the downstairs, and a dark-room was set up inside a closet. Julian had an office that he shared with Dottie Miller. Judging from the amount of paperwork they left behind, people like Mary King must have chained themselves to their typewriters. I was given an air travel credit card for Southern Airlines, and when events occurred or demonstrations broke out, I was rushed there by SNCC, usually at the request of Forman, in order to make pictures.

Soon after I made the pictures in Americus, a meeting of SNCC's executive committee was held in Atlanta. It was attended by important people whom I had never met—many from Howard University, which was a SNCC stronghold. I remember being introduced to Marion Barry and Courtland Cox by Forman as the new staff photographer when Barry said, "Why do we need him to take our pictures for us?" To my total disbelief, a discussion began as to whether or not SNCC could take its own pictures. Forman then took everyone into a small room—I think it was the bathroom—to discuss my fate. I had moved to Atlanta and thought I had been on the staff for months. Now, behind the closed door, they were discussing whether I should even be working for SNCC. I have never doubted that, inside that room, Forman used his considerable influence to create a place for me on the staff.

Washington, D.C.
August 28, 1963

SNCC chairman John Lewis speaks from the steps of the Lincoln Memorial.

James Baldwin and Marlon Brando at the Lincoln Memorial

SNCC members and friends defiantly gather to sing freedom songs.

Largely due to the frequent repetition of Dr. King's "I Have a Dream" speech on television, the March on Washington has become perhaps the single best-known event of the civil rights movement. People who were there at the time were less than enthusiastic about its importance. Ella Baker later said that "it was no protest." Sam Block, who had helped start the movement in Mississippi, called the march "the end of the movement." Julian Bond, who was assigned to help the dignitaries, spent much of that hot August afternoon with his arms plunged deep into a cooler of ice cubes, pulling out cold sodas. When Sammy Davis, Jr., said, "Thank you, boy," to Julian, it was simply too much for SNCC's poet and director of communications, who would have liked to answer, "Don't you 'boy' me, you ————!" But instead he went back to the ice water.

For those who had witnessed the movement in the Deep South, the march was not a very exciting event. I was lucky to find room to sleep on the floor of John's hotel room in the Statler-Hilton. The biggest thrill of the march for me was coming down the wide, red-carpeted steps of the hotel and stopping just above Malcolm X. A tall, handsome man with red hair, he was giving an impromptu press conference in the lobby. Later, in Detroit, Malcolm X gave his now famous "Grass Roots" speech in which he painted a vitriolic picture of the march: "They told those Negroes what time to hit town, how to come, where to stop, what sign to carry, what song to sing, what speech they could make and what speech they couldn't make and then told them to get out of town by sundown," which is not an inaccurate description of what happened.

John Lewis's speech was, in fact, censored. Such lines as "The party of Kennedy is also the party of Eastland. . . . Where is *our* party?" and "We will march through the South, through the heart of Dixie, the way Sherman did," apparently were unbearable to some members of the broad coalition that now rode the coattails of the movement. The fact that John and other members of SNCC had repeatedly risked their lives for the right to speak freely that day was not enough. Courtland Cox and Jim Forman took John into a bathroom inside the Lincoln Memorial and changed John's speech into a version acceptable to Patrick O'Doyle, the archbishop of Washington, who was refusing to appear on the podium with John. Whatever words he finally spoke, it was John himself that the young people were listening to that afternoon. He was one of them.

As if changing John's speech weren't enough, "We Shall Overcome" was left off the program because what everyone was really afraid of was a demonstration ("riot" in establishment parlance), and the powers that be thought the song would be provocative. So when the official program had ended and the untold tens of thousands of marchers were hustled off to their waiting buses, all the SNCC people, along with their wives, lovers, and friends, spontaneously started to sing. Because we were not "supposed" to do it, the singing became a brief moment of defiance. I was particularly annoyed when we got to "We Shall Overcome." As usual I could not hold hands and sing with everyone else. I had to step out and make a picture.

Exactly two weeks later, a member of the Klan placed a bomb under a stairway next to the basement of the Sixteenth Street Baptist Church in Birmingham, Alabama, timed to go off the next morning during Sunday school. It exploded on schedule, blowing the head entirely off one girl and also killing three others. They were all fourteen years old. That evening the Birmingham police killed another young black person, and two Eagle Scouts shot and killed a sixth young black as he was riding with a friend on a bicycle. I flew into Birmingham the next morning. Julian and John had already come in from Atlanta. More and more SNCC people arrived in what was really an SCLC town, everyone expecting demonstrations at the funeral for the four girls. Too many people were dying in the movement. Despite the hopes of the SNCC staff, nothing happened after the funeral.

A few days later, as I sat on a Southern Airlines plane waiting to fly out of Birmingham, one of the last passengers to board was Dr. King, who, with a small entourage, quickly walked down the aisle to the front of the plane, all of whose occupants were white. The passenger just across the aisle from me got very excited. "It's him. It's the coon." He couldn't control himself. He kept saying, "It's him. It's King. He's on the plane," as if he couldn't believe his eyes. It was an irresistible opportunity. I leaned way out across the aisle so that I could get really close to the man and then I said really loud, "Yes, sure enough, it's Martin Luther King. Isn't it an honor to be on the plane with him?" The man jumped up from his seat and left.

As the March on Washington ends, the SNCC staff and their friends gather to sing.

JOHN LEWIS
STUDENT NON-VIOLENT COORDINATING COMMITTEE, CHAIRMAN

We march today for jobs and freedom, but we have nothing to be proud of. For hundreds and thousands of our brothers are not here. They have no money for their transportation, for they are receiving starvation wages... or no wages, at all.

In good conscience, we cannot support the administration's civil rights bill, for it is too little, and too late. There's not one thing in the bill that will protect our people from police brutality. (We favorably call attention to the Kastenmeier Bill- H R. 7702.)

This bill will not protect young children and old women from police dogs and fire hoses, for engaging in peaceful demonstrations. This bill will not protect the citizens in Danville, Virginia, who must live in constant fear in a police state. This bill will not protect the hundreds of people who have been arrested on trumped-up charges. What about the three young men -- SNCC field secretaries -- in Americus, Georgia, who face the death penalty for engaging in peaceful protest?

The voting section of this bill will not help thousands of black citizens who want to vote. It will not help the citizens of Mississippi, of Alabama, and Goergia, who are qualified to vote, but lack a 6th Grade education. "One man, one vote," is the African cry. It is ours, too. (It must be ours.)

People have been forced to leave their homes because they dared to exercise their right to register to vote. What is in the bill that will protect the homeless and starving people of this nation? What is there is this bill to insure the equality of a maid who earns $5. a week in the home of a family whose income is $100,000   a year?

For the first time in 100 years this nation is being awakened to the fact that segregation is evil and that it must be destroyed in all forms. Your presence today proves that you have been aroused to the point of action.

We are now involved in a serious revolution. This nation is still a place of cheap political leaders who build their careers on immoral compromises and ally themselves with open forms of political, economic and social exploitation. What political leader here can stand up and say "My party is the party of principles"? The party of Kennedy is also the party of Eastland. The party of Javits is also the party of Goldwater. Where is our party?

In some parts of the South we work in the fields from sun-up to sun-down for $12 a week. In Albany, Goergia, nine of our leaders have been

(Above and following page) The original, uncensored speech of John Lewis

86

indicted not by Dixiecrats but by the Federal Government for peaceful protest. But what did the Federal Government do when Albany's Deputy Sheriff beat Attorney C.B. King and left him half-dead? What did the Federal Government do when local police officials kicked and assaulted the pregnant wife of Slater King, and she lost her baby?

It seems to me that the Albany indictment is part of a conspiracy on the part of the Federal Government and local politicians in the interest of political expediency.

Moreover, we have learned --and you should know -- since we are here for Jobs and Freedom -- that within the past ten days a spokesman for the Administration appeared in secret session before the committee that's writing the civil rights bill and opposed as has almost killed a provision that would have guaranteed in voting suits for the first time a fair federal district judges. And, I might add, this Administration's Bill, or any other civil rights bill -- as the 1960 civil rights act -- will be totally worthless when administered by racist judges, or many of whom have been consistently appointed by President Kennedy.

I want to know, which side is the Federal Government on?

The revolution is at hand, and we must free ourselves of the chains of political and economic slavery. The non-violent revolution is saying,

"We will not wait for the courts to act, for we have been waiting for hundreds of years. We will not wait for the President, the Justice Department, nor Congress, but we will take matters into our own hands and create a source of power, outside of any national structure that could and would assure us a victory." To those who have said, "Be Patient and Wait." we must say that, "Patience is a dirty and nasty work." We cannot be patient, we do not want to be free gradually, we want our freedom, and we want it now. We cannot depend on any political party, for both the Democrats and the Republicans have betrayed the basis principles of the Declaration of Independence. We all recognize the fact that if any radical social, political and economic changes are to take place in our society, the people, the masses, must bring them about. In the struggle we must seek more than mere civil rights; we must work for the community of love, peace and true brotherhood. Our minds, souls, and hearts cannot rest until freedom and justice exist for all the peeple.
The revolution is a serious one. Mr. Kennedy is trying to take the revolution out of the street and put it in the courts. Listen, Mr. Kennedy, Listen Mr. Congressman, listen fellow citizens, the black masses are on the march for jobs and freedom, and we must say to the politicians that there won't be a "cooling-off" period.
All of us must get in the revolution. Get in and stay in the streets of eve every city, every village and every hamlet of this nation, until true Freedom comes, until the revolution is complete. In the Delta of Mississippi, in southwest Georgia, in Alabama, Harlem, Chicago, Detroit, Philadelphia and all over this nation. -- the black masses are on the march!
We won't stop now. All of the forces of Eastland, Barnett, Wallace, and Thurmmond won't stop this revolution. The time will come when we will not confine our marching to Washington. We will march through the South, through the Heart of Dixie, the way Sherman did. We shall pursue our own "scorched earth" policy and burn Jim Crow to the ground -- nonviolently. We shall crack the South into a thousand pieces and put them back together in the image of democracy. We will make the action of the past few months look petty. And I say to you, WAKE UP AMERICA !!

Birmingham, Alabama
September 12, 1963

The morning after the bombing of the Sixteenth Street Baptist Church, heavily armed members of the Alabama Highway Patrol make a show of force near the church. The bomb exploded next to the wall and up through the floor of a Sunday school class. Four girls were buried in the bathroom and died.

The windows of the Sixteenth Street Baptist Church, where four fourteen-year-old girls were killed by a KKK bomb

Crowds wait along the funeral route.

Jimmy Hicks, Julian Bond, John Lewis, and Jeremiah X stand across the street from the bombed church.

People waiting in the street for the funeral of the murdered girls

Reverend Fred Shuttlesworth speaks at the funeral.

A grieving mourner enters the church for the funeral.

Dr. Martin Luther King just before he speaks at Birmingham

SNCC workers stand outside the funeral: Emma Bell, Dorie Ladner, Dona Richards, Sam Shirah, and Doris Derby.

Selma, October 7, 1963

Betty Mae Fikes

Until now, I had often been the only photographer and outsider in Deep South movement scenes. It was as if, as a journalist, I had the movement to myself. Now more and more people were coming south to be near SNCC. Alan Ribback came down from Chicago (he had owned the Gate of Horn nightclub where Lenny Bruce had often performed and had been arrested). Ribback brought with him sound recordist Robert McNamara, whose brother was already in the South as a photographer. Together, Ribback and McNamara wired the movement church in Selma, Alabama, for sound. They hung microphones from the ceiling on long wires as if they were working in Carnegie Hall. Ribback sat in the back with his Nagra III, wearing earphones. When fifteen-year-old Betty Mae Fikes led the Freedom Chorus, made up of high school kids, in "This Little Light of Mine," Ribback produced a recording that does more to capture the reality of the movement than almost any book I know.

The church was packed and steaming. Outside in the dark the police were waiting. No one was sure they could leave the church. Many of the children's friends were already in jail, kept in open compounds of barbed wire erected to contain their growing numbers. The clapping was like thunder as Betty Mae's great voice broke out high above the others: "This little light of mine, oh I'm gonna let it shine." Then she called out the names of their tormentors: "Go tell Al Lingo, I'm gonna let it shine," and the church roared. "Go tell Jim Clark, I'm gonna let it shine." Lingo was the notorious head of the Alabama Highway Patrol who favored electric cattle prods. Jim Clark was sheriff of Dallas County. (In a strange twist of justice, after bad check and mail fraud charges against him were dropped, Clark would serve two years in a federal prison in the late 1970s for smuggling marijuana.) Alan Ribback's recording was eventually issued as *Movement Soul*, a collection of songs and voices of the movement, and then released again as part of a Smithsonian collection of movement music put together by Bernice Reagon, who, as Bernice Johnson of Albany, had helped make freedom songs a fundamental part of the movement.

Sheriff Jim Clark arrests two demonstrators who displayed placards on the steps of the federal building in Selma. Howard Zinn, notebook in hand, appears in the final frame just behind Sheriff Clark.

James Baldwin addresses a packed mass meeting on Freedom Day.

SNCC's involvement in Selma began when Bernard Lafayette quietly moved there in 1962. On October 7, 1963, SNCC organized a Freedom Day, when hundreds of people stood in line all day waiting patiently to see the registrar. Jim Clark arrested two SNCC workers on federal property as they held up signs saying "Register to Vote." Since this event had been planned, I stood waiting at the steps to photograph the arrests. Once, when someone brought up my name at a Citizens Council meeting, Sheriff Clark stood up for me and said I was "okay," probably because I spent a lot of time talking with the police.

At one point Bernard Lafayette was almost murdered when a white man asked him to help fix a supposedly flat tire. As Lafayette bent over to look at the tire, he was struck in the head with a tire iron. When he stood up, his head streaming with blood, his would-be assassin stood ready to strike him again. Lafayette, a dedicated follower of King (and today the director of the Institute for Non-Violence in Albany, New York), looked the man right in the eye. Instead of hitting him again and probably killing him, the attacker backed off, and Lafayette survived. The movement he had helped start in Selma became big news two years later.

I left Selma with Julian Bond, using the small airport where Southern Airlines landed. In order to keep from drawing unwanted attention, Julian traveled as my servant. We loaded him down with all of my bags and all of his bags, while I strode up to the counter holding nothing and addressing him as "boy." I would say things like, "Now Julian, be careful with my bags," as he staggered around under the load and answered, "Yes, boss," and "No, boss." No one bothered us and we boarded the plane, having passed as either southerners of the old school or just two plain old lunatics.

Trying to register to vote, Dallas County citizens wait in line to see the registrar. Hundreds waited, but only a handful got inside.

An unlucky bystander falls into the hands of the law.

Selma on Saturday

Sheriff Jim Clark with his Dallas County deputies

Entrance to the City Cafe

The Freedom Choir in the Tabernacle Baptist Church. High school students and children helped start the Selma movement.

Mississippi
Fall 1963

The road to Yazoo City

A house in the Delta

Many times I made the long drive across Alabama into Mississippi. Bob Moses's romantic prediction from the Magnolia jail was indeed coming true. "This is a tremor in the middle of the iceberg—from a stone the builders rejected." The presence of young, black civil rights workers in the Deep and rural South had electrified communities. A large SNCC office was established in Greenwood, and on the next block, a Freedom House, where it was too noisy, too bright, and too crowded to sleep. When I wanted to be alone with a local girl, she told me to drive out and park at the edge of a cotton field, just behind the police station. "Are you sure this is a good spot to park?" I asked. The next morning, on the lawn of the Greenwood office, we examined the charred remains of a fiery cross that had burned there in the night. That fall the movement in Mississippi, now organized as COFO (the Council of Federated Organizations), ran Aaron Henry, the NAACP leader, and Ed King, a chaplain at Tugaloo, for governor and lieutenant governor in a mock election designed to give blacks a chance to vote and to dramatize the fact that they were excluded from voting in Mississippi.

Forman in the Greenwood SNCC office

A civil rights worker taking people trying to register to the Greenwood courthouse

Euvester Simpson and Willie Blue

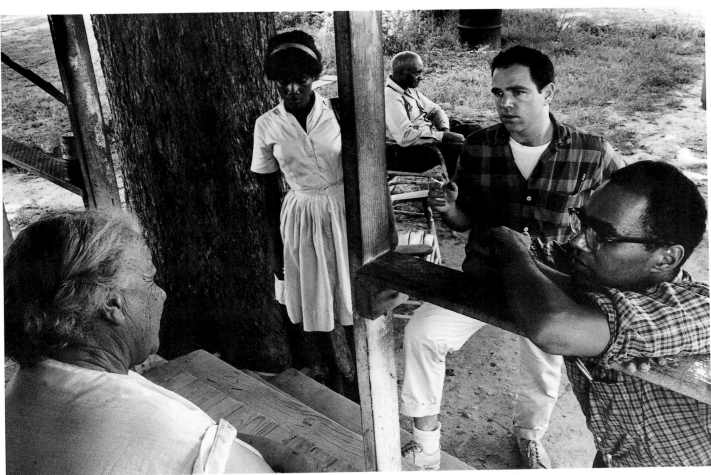

Martha Prescod, Mike Miller, and Bob Moses do voter registration work in the countryside.

The Clarksdale, Mississippi, police pose for a photograph as ministers from the National Council of Churches march to the local church.

After giving a concert in a cotton field in Greenwood, Bob Dylan plays behind the SNCC office. Bernice Reagon, one of the original Freedom Singers and today leader of Sweet Honey in the Rock, listens. Mendy Sampstein sits behind Dylan and talks to Willie Blue.

June Johnson in Clarksdale

Casey Hayden and John Lewis at a dance for the Aaron Henry gubernatorial campaign

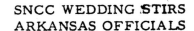

SNCC WEDDING STIRS
ARKANSAS OFFICIALS

PINE BLUFF, ARKANSAS - The marriage of two SNCC workers here

has been called "a deliberate, direct disservice to the white and colored

people of our state" by the State Attorney General.

Attorney General Bruce Bennet said of the newly-weds: "...neither

of these people works for a living, but are paid by the Student Nonviolent

Coordinating Committee, which is a trouble making organization."

The two - Mr. and Mrs. William Hansen - were married in

Cincinatti, Ohio on October 12.

Hansen is white. Mrs. Hansen, the former Ruthie Buffington, is a

Negro.

Interracial weddings are illegal in Arkansas.

Hansen has been in Pine Bluff since December, 1962. He helped

form the Pine Bluff Movement, and involved students at Arkansas

A & M in sit-in demonstrations. Mrs. Hansen, one of the students,

was, with ten others suspended from school on February 18.

Violation of the state's law against mixed marriages is punishable

by a fine and a one year jail sentence.

Both Hansen and his wife will remain in Pine Bluff. Both are SNCC

field secretaries.

Julian Bond, Bob Mants, and Julian's brother James, with his hand in front of his face, at the Zellners' wedding

William Hansen and the former Ruthie Buffington

Rickie Green and Chuck McDew in New York

Bob Zellner and Dottie Miller get married in Atlanta.

Southwest Georgia, 1963

Charles Sherrod (standing at right) and Randy Battle (seated) visit a supporter in the Georgia countryside.

Sherrod married there and thirty years later is still in southwest Georgia, a member of the Albany City Council.

Ralph Allen in Terrill County

An Albany gang leader who has become a movement activist

Charles Sherrod

Eddie Brown in Americus, Georgia

Atlanta
November 22, 1963

I was driving into the office from our apartment late one morning when I stopped at a small grocery store to get a soda. A black man leaned into the open window of my Oldsmobile and mumbled, "You killed the President." He seemed drunk. Inside the store the volume on the radio was turned way up.

The real concern at the Atlanta office was what the assassination of President Kennedy would do to SNCC and the movement. What if a black man had done it? What forces would be unleashed against the people in that room? The resulting discussion survives in minutes taken by Mal Clissold. These notes are a window into the past, unclouded by all the politics and mythmaking that have intruded between that day and now. Look how aggressive SNCC appears as Sam Shirah says, "This is the time to take the offensive." Kennedy is no hero to these people, and his position on civil rights is felt to be a result of pressure created by the movement and the people in the room. Everyone participates in the discussion; all are equals. Many suggest that the event should be used to urge passage of the civil rights bill "as a memorial," which is in fact what happened. Forman—always political, always a strategist, always a teacher—warns them that they should only call for something that they know they can carry out.

The final statement, which illustrates one of SNCC's core strengths, invokes the "moral sword" that Diane Nash had introduced to America in 1961: "We must always remember that at the end the highest considerations are moral principles."

I will always remember that the very tense afternoon ended with Forman breaking out in song. Standing in that second-floor room of the Marx Building, everyone began to sing, and then they really began to sing. For years I believed the photograph reproduced on page 123 was made at that moment, but too many people—Mike Thelwell, John Lewis, Julian Bond, Lawrence Guyot, Judy Richardson, Jean Wheeler—in the picture are not mentioned in the notes of the discussion, so it could not have been made on the same day. The photograph shows everyone singing in the same room, so it was probably made during one of the Atlanta conferences, which would have brought everyone into town.

Below and on the following pages are minutes of the discussion in the Atlanta office on the afternoon and evening of President Kennedy's assassination.

FRIDAY AFTERNOON

The telegram to the brother of the president was read.

---It was suggested that Kennedy's postuse was a "contribution." His action was not "momentous."

---Clissold said that the discussion should cover the future--what Johnson will do, whether he will protect or attack SNCC.

Nancy---She suggested that the discussion should cover the influence this will have on the next election. She asked, What can you expect from Johnson.

Forman---Rember that Dallas is the stronghold of the rightists. This trip was to bolster Johnson.

Nancy---This act is typical of our demented society. It is not isolated, and we should present it as such.

---This is a reactionary act, a conservative act. We must beware of the "deeper emergency" which this act dramatizes.

Ivanhoe---We must decide what we will do in Washington. Anything? The reaction of the field worker may be: "If they can kill Kennedy-- me too?" The cops in Mississippe may consider this a go ahead for more killing. Will they think that liberalism is dead when the man is dead.

---Whatever Kenndey did on behalf of Civil Rights was because there was a pressure group demanding action. We must continue pressure.

Sandy---This may also initiate a counteraction with more pressure on the reactionary forces. If no one is safe, more stringent measures may be necessary.

Alan---Send a statement to the Justice Dept. urging strict measures.

Nancy---This could also be used to curb SNCC.

---This shows the danger when we wire.

---We must never forget, even during the President's death, to determine what SNCC's role is in the social revolution.

Forman---The point is to determine how to interpert the death of the president. I interpert it as a national problem -- like the death's of the four girls in Birmingham and Medgar Evers -- which must be used as a symbol. It is not a signal to wait.

Factual information on the assination was given.

Several points were made: 1. Possibly this will initiate a
crack down on unpopular radical organizations. 2. His death could
be a unifying factorin which all factions would support the passage
of the civil rights bill. The Civil Rights Organizations should
continue to push for the adaption of the program which they approve.
The alternative is to be quiet and moderate.

Reagon----Suggestion for an overnight vigil at Lincoln Memorial while
SNCC is in Washington.

Alan----Suggestion for a memorial to Kennedy to be proposed by the
Civil Rights Organizations.

Reagon----Whatever Kennedy did for Civil Rights was because of pressure
groups. This pressure must continue.

Nancy----You can not bring in the social issue of a demented society
as well now that the man who shot him is accused of being leftist.

Shira----This is the time to take the offensive. Above all, we are
non-violent. This act is a symtom of a disease. We "must take action
to eliminate the disease which would produce these symptoms."
He called for demonstrations on college campuses throughtout the nation.

Debbie----Try to exploit every aspect of his bill for our advantage.

Nancy----Concentrate onthe man and what he did, not on the killing.

Forman----Sam's point was the large context of non-violence.

a CNVA peace walker----The United States has had much to do with violent
tactics, as exemplified by South Vietnam. It is very important to
get into the streets, soon.

Forman----We should demonstrate mournfully when we demonstrate, with
black suits and arm bands. Kennedy wanted a Civil Rights Bill. We
have an obligation to push the program for the public image. We
must be disciplined, dignified, and respectful.
There is no more fitting memorial to Kennedy than the passage of his
Civil Rights Bill.

Tom----The southern students and workers will have a chance to express
t eir ideas at the Washington conference.

Forman----Johnson is taking over now, without hesitation. We can not
be shocked, it slows our intellect. We can't delay.

★ ★ ★

Shira----We must speak out, now.

Prince----From experience in this field, he knows that sentimentality
can mess you up terribly. SNCC can not lose a week because of sentimentality
In reality, SNCC does not have an element of control in the situation.
Nor do we have all the facts. In this case as in others, sentimentswill
develope either negatively or psoitively. Then, no matter how demonstrations
occur and are conducted, "we could kick off a race war." We must think
of the consequences. Think carefully, then act.

Fox----He doubts whether the majority of the population will be against
demonstrations.

Ruby Doris Smith, James Forman, Marion Barry, and Sam Shirah at the SNCC Washington conference shortly after Kennedy's death

Mark----He disagrees. The Establishment may be against any type of demonstrations. He fears a major purge of the leftist elements.

Ivanhoe----The fact this is an election year will stabalize circumstances and prevent a purge. This is not McCarthy time.

Dinky----His death will worsen the situation.

Forman----We are confusing two issues which must be kept separate.
1. We have a legitmate interest in working the the backward areas.
Therefor we must: a. Ask for passage of the Civil Rights legislation.
b. Conduct demonstrations in a dignified manner, respectfully. We can research Kennedy's speeches relative to his civil rights position, and use his quotes.
2. What will this do to the left. While this is important, it should be kept separate for the other issue.

Dinky--Only by taking the offensive will we prevent a purge.

Forman----The rightist and birchists etc. will attempt to use this killing against the Civil Rights Organizations. We must take a <u>positive</u> stand.

----Anyone left of center will be subject to a purge. We must take stand, stand up.

Forman----Johnson will use this against the Civil Rights Organizations.

Cobb----Mississippi is always bad and this will hardly make it worse.
What is important is the rest of the country and how it will react.

Forman----They will link the demonstration with the man who killed Kennedy.

Ivanhoe----The people who the worker try to reach will be afraid. The Establishment of Miss. will be just as hostile.

Shira----We are on the defensive, true. But the best defensive will be a strong offensive. While the country is in shcok, we should come on with a strong offensive.

★   ★   ★

Mark----You should always understand the abstract, future dangers and the specific immediate action. Keep them separate, but keep both in mind.

Cordell----We will be in Washington. We can capitalize on this situation.

Iris----The Student Voice is a good idea, but do not make Kennedy into something he was not.

John Ball----Lets get down to work, something constructive.

----The vigil is a good idea. If it is carried out for nationwide publicity the left will not be as subject to purge. The identification will be with Kennedy, not with his killer.

Sandy----He spoke about and clarified several issues: 1. The Civil Rights Movement will receive a negative response from the Federal Government, the Press, and the local people. 2. To correct this, get the Voice out, support Kennedy, and encourage further legislation.
3. The whole conference should participate in the vigil in Washington.
4. Don't forget. Friday there is a press conference, which is the time to get to the press exactly SNCC's opinions.

Boy next to Iris---I do not want to demonstrate for a guy who sold out on Civil Rights, not demonstrate as if he had not sold out.

Cordell---I respect Kennedy beaause he was president, not just any guy. I demonstrate in this respect.

Dinky---I wan to use him and his death, not eulogize him. 2. The Establishment will oppose us under any circumstances. We must act, not be afraid.

Forman---Cordell should not have backed down and changed his position. I was surpirsed the killer was not a rightst. Because he is a leftist, we can not take the position this was the same thing that killed Evers. We must take the position he died a martyer's death, like the others. Demonstrations will occur for the monument of legislation, not for the president alone.
We can save our statements for Washington. No use to speak to soon. You should call for only what you can carry out, always.

---After all our political discussion on tactics and polimcy, we must always remember that at the end, the hightest considerations are moral principles.

James Forman leads singing in the SNCC office on Raymond Street in Atlanta. (From left) Mike Sayer, McArthur Cotton, Forman, Marion Barry, Lester MacKinney, Mike Thelwell, Lawrence Guyot, Judy Richardson, John Lewis, Jean Wheeler, and Julian Bond

Atlanta, Winter 1963–1964

That Atlanta was home to the main SNCC office was a special curse to the city, for in addition to putting up with the local movement, the city had to survive the South's most militant and experienced organizers when they used it as their winter home. Conferences that brought fieldworkers into town also sparked marches, arrests, and sit-ins.

One target for such protests was Leb's, a Jewish delicatessen in the heart of the city that sported Star of David decals and long kosher salamis hanging in the window. At that time, I was used to the idea of Jews being the oppressed, not the oppressors, and the sight of blintzes and kosher food being used to defend segregation was too much for me. Scuffles would break out in the glass entranceway. As I stood inside watching Mr. Lebowitz slamming the demonstrators repeatedly with the glass door, I lost control of myself and yelled out, "You're just like the Nazis!" At that point he stopped slamming the demonstrators and started slamming the door on me.

Outside in the street, an act was occurring that helped restore my faith in humanity. About twenty students had sat down in the intersection, holding signs that protested segregation and discrimination in hiring and making it impossible to drive down the street. A mob gathered, and a few demented people began to torment the students. One would go up and pull their hair and their ears. Others would kick them and stick burning cigarettes on them. A white woman, holding a ream of typing paper, just happened to be walking up the street, and she stepped into the midst of the mob, verbally accosting the most aggressive people. "You should be ashamed of yourselves," she yelled at them. "What's the matter with you?" In all the confrontations I had witnessed or would witness, I cannot ever recall anything similar happening. The crowd hesitated, then stopped completely as the woman continued her tongue-lashing. Single-handedly, and using only words, she had subdued a mob of men. There was a pause. Then from the back of the crowd someone yelled, "If you feel that way, why don't you marry one of them?" And everyone laughed. The heroine with the ream of paper sat down and joined the demonstrators.

A driver attacks a demonstrator blocking traffic.

Forman is arrested near Leb's Restaurant.

As demonstrators block traffic to protest segregation and unfair hiring practices in downtown Atlanta, a mob begins to abuse them with kicks, blows, and burning cigarettes. An anonymous woman walking by with a box of typing paper confronts the mob and for a while holds them at bay. When someone yells, "If you feel that way, why don't you marry one of them?" she sits down and joins the demonstrators.

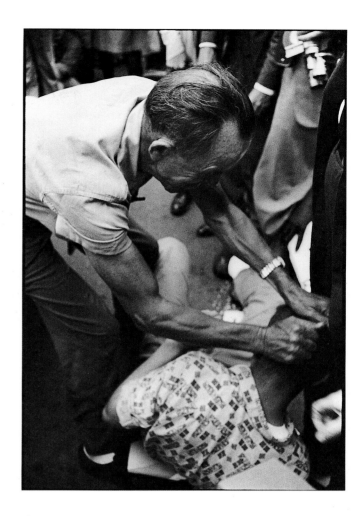

One of high school student Taylor Washington's numerous arrests is immortalized as he yells while passing before me. The photograph became the cover of SNCC's photo book, The Movement, *and was reproduced in the former Soviet Union in* Pravda, *captioned "Police Brutality USA."*

A Toddle House in Atlanta has the distinction of being occupied during a sit-in by some of the most effective organizers in America when the SNCC staff and supporters take a break from a conference to demonstrate. Included in these pictures are Dick Gregory, Willie Ricks, Joyce Ladner, Taylor Washington, Judy Richardson, Chico Neblett, Stokely Carmichael, Charlie Cobb, George Green, James Forman, Courtland Cox, and Marion Barry.

Hattiesburg, Mississippi
January 22, 1964

Lafayette Surney (second from left) and Gwen Gillom (far right) flank demonstrators on the steps of the Forrest County Courthouse during Freedom Day. (Bottom) Oscar Chase talks with Dorie Ladner. Chase, one of two people arrested that day, was beaten by police in jail. The next day Howard Zinn and two attorneys took Chase, still with a bloody shirt, swollen face, and smashed nose, to the local FBI office. The FBI agent looked at the journalist, the two attorneys, and Chase and said, "Who was it got the beating?"

Demonstrators in Hattiesburg

Hattiesburg's finest arrive to supervise Freedom Day.

The second person arrested that day, Bob Moses, is taken away to jail.

Fannie Lou Hamer, sharecropper from a family of twenty children, evicted from her home for applying to register to vote, severely beaten in the Winona police station, SNCC field secretary from Ruleville, and future Mississippi Freedom Democratic party candidate for Congress, marches in the cold Hattiesburg rain.

The movement office in Clarksdale

That night Dona Richards, Euvester Simpson, and Gwen Gillom sing on the courthouse steps.

Feb. 12, 1964

Dear Mom and Dad,

I could not help but think that the underscoring of Rustin's beliefs meaned that you thought they might apply to me. I wish they did, for I agree with him and would not hesitate to go home or back to Chicago, or many other places I'd rather be. I've finished with my work for the book and remain here because I have to. I'm very involved in the SNCC organization and doubt if I would be so easily replaced. I'd rather be making a movie or money or generally enjoying myself which is the main thing I don't get to do in the South. For someone that fits into the movement, which even Northerners can do if they're around long enough, to leave, is generally regarded as traitorous; or anyway a kind of retreat morally. I don't know if thats true but it is part of the ethic down here.

Frankly I'd love to leave. I'd like to go to New York and hobnob with people how dig my pictures or go to Chicago and be with my friends. This mood comes on me every two months or so and is the thing that sent me home on these occassions when I left the South this summer. The trouble is I always come back, because I want to and because I feel I have to. And then of course after some weeks the same thing happens again.

In many ways I think that the things I do here are good for me to use a poor term. I have responsibility in my work here, which frankly I hate. Somehow, because of the movement and the conditions of the country I feel forced to face that responsibility. In the particular form it means doing SNCC pamphlets instead of rding and photographing motrocycles. I am very awear that the lure of New York is the lure of fun and irresponsibility. To just do things that are fun for the cause means very little to oneself. In general I seem to believe that to leave SNCC would be to turn away from the movement. Today John Lewis sat over diner with me and said what a waste of time this all was. He ment all the work all of us are doing. None of us want to be here. Forman would like to be writing, John wants to go to Africa and they all really want to leave, but can't of course. The system remains, segregation has not yet fallen, only vicotries keep everyone here. I guess they keep me here, my little victories, as a kind of substitue for the enjoyment of the North. The Danville pamphlet, a poster that makes money for SNCC, even selling pictures and passing the check on to SNCC; these things have, for a brief moment given me a satisfaction preveously unknown to me.

I don't think I'll stay forever, in fact as I keepsaying I'd like to try something else; eventually I'll make of my mind as to what that is and I'll leave. For a while anyway.

Love,

Danny

My mother used to clip articles from the New York Times *and send them to me if she thought I ought to be interested. Bayard Rustin, who organized the March on Washington, had published a letter saying that whites in the movement ought to organize in the white northern communities. My answer to my parents is reproduced above.*

Cambridge, Maryland, Spring 1964

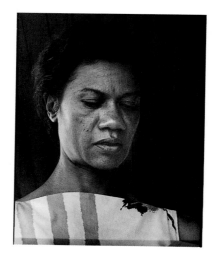

Gloria Richardson

Cambridge, Maryland, was the northernmost of the SNCC outposts. It was known for its militancy and for the power of the woman who led the movement there, Gloria Richardson. For much of the spring of 1964, Cambridge was occupied by the Maryland National Guard. During one night march, the guard stopped the marchers on the edge of the white community. I've never much cared for the dark, didn't own a flash, and would take pictures at night by leaning on a wall and making time exposures or by just shooting when a TV cameraman turned on his lights. That night Clifford Vaughs, who was from California and had recently begun to make pictures for SNCC, handed me his flash, saying he didn't need it because he was going to be arrested. People were sitting down in the street. Someone hurled a bottle toward the guard troops, and Gloria Richardson mounted a National Guard jeep to ask for calm. Then the guard tried to arrest Clifford, and a tug-of-war developed as demonstrators held Clifford's feet while the guard pulled him away.

I wasn't sure where to stand. The guard had fixed bayonets, then they had brought forward a man who looked like a vacuum-cleaner salesman from outer space. He had two huge tanks of gas on his back and a large hose in his hands. All the guardsmen were donning their gas masks. There were quite a few journalists present, and they all crossed over to the guard and stood behind the line of soldiers. I went and stood with the demonstrators. Then the soldier with the tank of gas went to work. A huge cloud of pepper gas enveloped us. I felt like someone had just stepped on my eyeballs. It was really painful, and I staggered away into the darkness as the crowd scattered, hardly able to see. I turned and made a single, hopeless exposure of the big white cloud settling down on some remaining protesters. Wandering through the back streets of the Negro community, I heard the occasional "pop" of gunfire. The guard was marching down the street, spraying gas everywhere. Inside one of the houses, an infant died of asphyxiation. I had always thought I could use my wits to protect myself in the movement. But how do you protect yourself from gunfire?

Stokely Carmichael, then twenty-two years old, was seated at the very front of the line of demonstrators, and the gas was sprayed directly into his face. He must have suffered terribly. That night most of the staff went to visit him at the hospital.

Another day, I was returning from a demonstration in Annapolis with John Lewis, and the car was packed with SNCC people, including Stokely. I was driving and playing Roy Orbison loudly on the radio when a long arm reached over from the back seat and changed the station. "How can you listen to that honky shit?" It was Stokely.

Stokely Carmichael and the Maryland National Guard

Gloria Richardson, Stokely Carmichael, and Cleve Sellers in custody in Cambridge, Maryland

Clifford Vaughs, another SNCC photographer, is arrested by the National Guard.

A cloud of pepper gas descends on the marchers.

Reggie Robinson attends to demonstrators who have been gassed.

A march through the Maryland night

An angry crowd forms in Cambridge.

Atlanta, June 10, 1964
Staff Meeting

Prathia Hall

In June a staff meeting was held in Atlanta. In the minutes of that meeting, held Wednesday, June 10, the discussion has been preserved. Again we step into the past. No one in the room knows the future. Often without funds, but not powerless, they themselves are shaping the future. A single issue is being discussed: the presence of guns inside the Greenwood, Mississippi, SNCC office. How long can SNCC lead a nonviolent movement when its members and the people they hope to lead are more and more subjected to violence? As a number of people mention, guns have always been around the movement. Prathia Hall makes an amazing speech, still moving and eloquent across time, even though we are reading only an abbreviation of what she said. "We are fighting here because we want life to be worth living." When she adds that we will "bring our blood to the White House door," Ruby Doris correctly points out that *nothing* happened after the murder of the children in Birmingham. Everyone expects murders in Mississippi that summer when one thousand student volunteers, many of them white, arrive for the summer project. Prathia says, "We must improve our communications so we won't lose a man without knowing it." In less than two weeks they will lose three. Communications will still be so bad that, unbeknownst to SNCC, the three will be held prisoner in a local jail for hours while the Klan gathers their executioners. This time, though, the White House will act, largely because two of the victims are white.

Nor could the group be tougher on itself. Complaints are made about people being "comfortable" and spending too much money for gas and food.

Another issue is not on the table but is in the room. Charles MacLaurin, who two years earlier was walking the dusty streets of Ruleville as part of an all-black group of fieldworkers, asks when SNCC will take the issue of nonviolence into the *white* community. Noting that whites working in the Negro community are often attacked he says, "Whites should develop within the white, not Negro, community." It is an issue that will return to haunt SNCC and that will never be resolved.

Sam Block

Charles MacLaurin

Charlie Cobb

Hollis Watkins

Don Harris

Lawrence Guyot

Mike Sayer

(Below) The minutes from the Wednesday morning, June 10, meeting of the staff in Atlanta. The photographs of the participants were made in the field, not at the meeting.

Report from 2nd congressional district: Mississippi

James Jones;
Notes first that staff has been in ⌷Greenwood a very long time⌷ On March 24 a cross was burned near the office and they received phoned threats. The decision was made to protect the people around the office and to prevent people breaking in and bombing it.

Charlie Cobb:
Concerning guns in the office; they were there for two reasons: 1)people were breaking in for food and clothes. 2)whites are organizing in vigilante groups. A truckload of guns was stopped in Clinton, Illinois, and the feeling is that the truck was originally headed for Mississippi. Amizie Moore was told by a white that he, Mrs. Hamer, Moses, and Aaron Henry were slated to be killed. The feeling is that violence this summer will be directed at black staff members and leaders and not at white summer volunteers. Staff members felt they would be killed. They got guns for the house and the office with the idea of self defense, to protect against the organized violence which is developing.

Chalres MacLaurin: Throughout the second district people are arming themselves.

Guyot:
Also, the sheriff rides around and asks people not to house summer project and tells them not to repeat the conversations to Mrs. Hamer.
Jones failed to stamp out ideas brought in by outside groups, killing formerly workable ways

Ruby: The outside group Guyot is refering to is RAM (Revolutionary Afro-American Movement). Max Stanford, of RAM, came into Mississippi and has exerted a great deal of influence there.

Willie Peacock: People in the 2nd district have advised us to arm. The office was broken into, and there is the fear that it could happen again and a bomb could be planted. They have ordered Sanders (the landlord) to shoot at anyone breaking into the office, but he said he wouldn't. Peacock therefore inniated the idea of guns being brought in, and they have been there since January. Access to the Freedom House is through two alleys and it would be easy for someone to sneak in and break into the house. County people say they are going to defend themselves because they know the whites are not playin g. They have set up a self defense structure so that if there is violence in an area anyone there must make an account of his presence. The FBI was unwilling to track down the guilty parties in the shooting last year. That means the whites are sure they can kill a Negro and get away with it.
Peacock feels that when he and the other four were beaten in jail in Starksville that they could have been taken to the county farm without anyone knowing it.

Hollis Watkins: He noted a change since he was working in Mississippi. People had guns in their houses then too; they were protecting their hom es. Things have changed, however. There was a nonviolent attitude then. As to proecting the office, if we were guarding it because of the food and clothing then they should be moved.

Dick Frey: At the present the Greenwood staff is totally demoralized. There is little movement in the town and the feeling for the Movement has gone down. Nobody has been effectively leading the project, assigning responsibilities or giving program ideas. SNCC staff is leading a comfortable life in Greenwood but is not giving anything to the community. People throughout SNCC know this. Is the defense in Greenwood a defense against outside powers or against our own incompetance?

Don Harris: People are being shot in areas other than Mississippi. Las month a young boy was shot in Albany by a policeman. He was shot on a Saturday night. On Monday night 1200 people came to a mass meeting. They were mad. Young people and people on the frigges of the movement were expressing themselves. That night they could have had as big a demnstration or blow-up as ever. But they talked nonviolence and it cut the meeting immediately. Some people put us down because of it. Don now asks - what right we have to stop these people from doing what they want to do.

Willie Peacock: What Frey said of Greenwood is true. People are frustrated because of lack of money. Machines need repairs: cars, mimeos, etc. They feel that everything takes priority over Leflore County. They feel that SNCC is unwilling to give them money, and their credit is runied. They have some bills which are 4 or 5 months old. When they were beaten in Starksville no one knew and no one cared.

Miss Baker: Questioned how the project could run up $500 gas bill and
               $400 food bill.
               Answer: Gas and food bills were primarily an accumulation of
               debts. Gas was high partially because of freedom day, and
               partially because people passing through the Delta use Greenwood
               as a way station.

Ruby Doris: We have personnel and staff problems in all projects. People
               are irresponsible because we've allowed them to be so and left
               them in the projects.
               Re self defense: in 1961 people had arms, but nothing was made
               of it. The objectives conditions have been changed since then.
               We are asking people to expose themselves to more and more.
               In Cambridge, Md. we have taken people onto the streets, stirred
               them up, and then turned them back with talk of nonviolence.

Don Harris: We are exposing people to more dangers all the time. We are not
               acting quickly enough for our own people. Willie Ricks was in
               jail for 30 days and no one lifted a finger to get the money
               to get him out.

Frank Smith: We are telling people from the north in their orientation sessions
               for Mississippi that they must stay alive when they get to the
               state. We are fighting the structure of Mississippi with only
               our bodies and souls. The people going to Mississippi with the
               idea that they might be beaten, shot, and might have to stay
               in jail. People can't always know where we are. There is no
               protection against Mississippi. That's what we're fighting
               for. Only the Federal government can protect us and it won't.
               If we concentrate only on staying alive, people will be too
               frightened to cross the street.

Sam Block: During the past month whites have been more threatening than
               ever. Three months ago a white man came to the office and
               said he'd be back in the middle of the night with police. That
               night a shot was fired by the office and a private plane circled
               the office. The office was told that the man flying had wanted
               to bomb the office but had been deterred.
               Mrs. McGee's house was almost bombed—she has guns and has been
               able to stop some violence. What are we to say to her.

Courtland: The problem of defense goes beyond Mississippi. Negroes in
               New York are becoming increasingly aggressive. In Cambridge
               possibilities of violence are increasing. Our people are afraid
               for their lives. To the extent that we think of our own lives
               we are politically immobilized. We volunteer for this situation
               knowing what's happening and we must accept the implications.
               Self defense can only maintain the status quo, it can't change
               the existing situation.

Charlie Cobb: We will be living on a farm with a man who has guns. What
               would happen if someone attacked his house and he shot back.
               If Charlie were there would SNCC stand by him, even though
               SNCC advocates nonviolence.

Willie Blue: It's very difficult to define our situation. We don't know
               how far we will let the man push us before we defend ourselves.
               It's a personal thing.

Minutes: Wednesday June 10, 1964

Prathia Hall: Nothing said so far has been invalid. No one can be rational about death. For the first time we are facing that this _may_ be the last time. We are fighting because we want life to be worth living. When I discovered I was dead already I decided That I'd die to gain life.
We must improve our communications so that we won't lose a man without knowing it. As for staying in jail, it's demoralizing to be in jail and feel that no one cares, but that is what we're here for. How can we defend our lives except by fighting for them. When the kids in Birmingham were killed I wanted to pick up a gun until I realized that by destroying lives we don't preserve them. I can't take a life knowingly. We talk of a man defending his home. If you kill an atacker ourside the window you lose your home anywqy because the townsmen will come to the defense of the attacker and take everything from you. We must just bring the reality of our situation to the nation. Bring our blood on to the white house door. If we die here it's the whole society which has pulled the trigger by its silence. How much can we deal with self defense. We can deal with the specifics of communication and our responsibilities within our program. Concerning funds, when we came down we knew we didn't have a dime, and if we think the country will give us money to turn it upside down we're crazy. When we started raising cain in Atlanta the next week the money began to stop coming in. We're idealistic if we think that people will give us money to take it out of their pockets.

Ruby Doris: We know that the summer project was conceived with the idea that there would be bloodshed, but what does it mean to say that violence will be brought to the doorstep of the White House. No one in Brimingham rose after the shootings and bombings. There was no program. If we must pperate off the land like guerillas we must function that way.

Mike Sayer: In Monroe, N.Carolina men defend their homes with guns. The Klan drove through and were shot at and they didn't gome back. Defending your home is dignity. We can't assume what reaction will take place to self defense. We dan't be sure it won't lead to a holocost. The way the situayion exists now whites know that violence is the most sensible way of getting us.

MacLaurin: When are we going into the white community with the idea of nonviolence.

Mendy Samstein: Ed Hamlett is developing programs with about 25 southern whites. It's difficult to develop such a program. Note that when the whites hit McComb they were immediately beaten.

MacLaurin: When whites come down they rush into the Negro community. That's why they're beaten. Whites should develop within the white, not Negro community.

Mississippi Summer, 1964

Gwen Gillom, a staff member from Alabama, conducts a literacy class in Ruleville.

the freedom news

VOL. I NO.1   July 8, 1964

HOW WE FEEL ABOUT THE THREE MISSING BOYS.

The news just suddenly broke out as a shock. The people were scared and angry, saying "Why would any person want to take the lives of the three boys."

The people in the country were scared and some were even scared to come to town. I feel sorry for those boys and I think they should be found. The missing boys were a shock to some. The white wasn't so sad.

They found their station wagon. It was burned. Some people think they are dead. Some say the police are not looking as hard as they should be and most people think they cut them up in little pieces and threw them in the river.

By Frances Lee Jeffries

An excerpt from a newsletter written and published by the Freedom School in Holly Springs

By the summer of 1964, I wanted to leave SNCC. Until then, I had enjoyed being the only photographer at many of the places SNCC had sent me. Now more and more photographers were coming to SNCC. Matt Heron, a *Black Star* photographer, had moved to Atlanta with his family and had begun to organize a documentary photo project within SNCC. I hated being organized and even argued that what was now happening in the movement did not lend itself to photography. The politics of the movement were complicated. Photography dealt with surfaces.

There was another reason to leave. Some movement people didn't think whites should be there at all, and this thought, once left unspoken, was coming out into the open more and more. I recall the first time in the Atlanta office I heard Ruby Doris say that whites shouldn't be there. It was as though a Pandora's box had opened. And once it opened, nothing would close it back up. In Nashville, after a SNCC conference on the Fisk campus, a small group including John Lewis and me went over to a meeting of black nationalists that was going on simultaneously on the campus. Only when we got there, I was told that, being white, I was not welcome inside the room. A table at the entrance was covered with movement and black nationalist literature, some reproducing my photographs on their covers. I know John wanted to go inside, but he didn't. As the others from the SNCC conference took their seats, John turned and, in solidarity with me, left the room.

Plans for the Mississippi Summer of 1964 had been extremely controversial within SNCC. One thousand mostly white college students from the North, Midwest, and West were brought to the state to work for the movement. Freedom Schools were set up in most areas of the state, usually in rural communities. Voter registration work was done everywhere. Overnight the project created an integrated and culturally diverse community deep in the Black Belt, and in that sense it was a utopian event, wonderful and historic. But it also drew most of SNCC's forces into and focused all its attention on Mississippi, despite years of work in other communities. It brought a high infusion of whites into a black movement that included integration among its ideals, though few on the staff doubted that public social integration in rural Mississippi would be deadly.

As soon as the summer project began—actually, the week before it began—three of the workers were taken into the southeast Mississippi woods and murdered by the Ku Klux Klan. I was in New York City when news came that the three civil rights workers were missing. I knew right away that they were dead, and so did everyone else. It was Andy Goodman's death that rattled me the most. Goodman, a summer volunteer from New York, had gotten into a car with CORE workers James Chaney and Mickey Schwerner to go take a look at a burned-down church near Philadelphia in Neshoba County. I had been doing that sort of thing all along. Like the gunfire I had heard in Cambridge, Maryland, the death of the three workers unnerved me. I wanted to photograph the movement, but I didn't want to die doing it. Along with Dottie and Julian, I had produced the "Mississippi Summer" pamphlets that had brought the students to the South. Feeling that I really didn't have any choice, that night I returned to Mississippi.

I joined one of the groups in the small Delta town of Ruleville, home of Fannie Lou Hamer—the place where I had met Charlie Cobb and Frank Smith two years earlier. I lived along with other volunteers in rooms in Rene Williams's home; she would go out the back door and pick what looked like weeds from her garden and cook them for our dinner. Probably because she was housing summer volunteers, we got pieces of chicken to eat now and then.

When I wasn't in Ruleville that summer, I was driving around the state in my Oldsmobile. At a Freedom School in southeast Mississippi, I ran into Jane Stembridge, and together we decided to go to the Neshoba County Fair near Philadelphia. A Neshoba County sheriff who was a member of the Klan had helped murder Schwerner, Goodman, and Chaney. The sheriff's posse also ran the county fair. So it was a strange place for SNCC's first employee and a staff photographer to go for recreation, but people did strange things back then. Dottie Miller once told me that Mike Sayer, a white SNCC staff member, used to go to meetings of the Ku Klux Klan.

I was spending my time at the fair taking pictures of a girl who ran one of the games when I noticed a lot of people watching me. I walked off toward the corrals of goats and sheep and unloaded my camera, replacing what I had just shot with a blank roll of film. As I tried to leave, a group of sheriff's men surrounded me and told me to give them the film. Even though it was broad daylight and there were people all around, I was terrified. One of the men said, "What happened to those boys is gonna happen to you," a strange comment since at that point Schwerner, Goodman, and Chaney were officially listed only as "missing." I wasn't about to argue with them. I unloaded my camera and gave them the blank roll of film I had just put into it, and they let me go. It took a lot to keep from running flat out for my car, but I got there fast enough, and all I could think of was that I hoped Jane Stembridge was around. She must have seen what had happened, because she was standing by the car when I got to it. I drove for twenty miles without taking my eyes off the rearview mirror, going as fast as I could out of Neshoba County, never happier to see the empty road stay empty as it disappeared behind me.

During the hunt for Goodman, Schwerner, and Chaney, the searchers kept finding other bodies that they weren't looking for. One was a torso pulled from the river, bound up with wire. Later that summer, before they found the three workers' bodies, I flew back to New York from Memphis. At the airport I talked with a CORE worker who was also leaving the state, a black man all decked out in overalls, which was a movement uniform. Someone noticed us and must have telephoned the FBI, for when I landed that night at LaGuardia, my mother was waiting for me, and right behind her was a man in a gray hat and trench coat. "Are you Mickey Schwerner?" he asked. "I'm from the Federal Bureau of Investigation." (Bob Zellner still calls them the Federal Bureau of Intimidation.) "No," I answered. "I'm Danny Lyon. This is my mother." "That's not good enough," he shot back. "Got any identification?" The alert citizen who had watched me talking to the CORE worker at the Memphis airport had apparently called the bureau to report that Schwerner and Chaney had emerged from hiding and were about to leave the state. Oh, how I wish they had.

The picture from the Neshoba County Fair that I rescued from the sheriff's posse

The Mississippi Freedom Democratic party was created in 1964 as an alternative to the regular state parties, from which blacks were excluded. Eighty thousand people joined. Here people vote in Mississippi, most for the first time in their lives.

HEAR! HEAR!
HOW OUR BROTHERS
Died For Freedom
AND HOW WE ARE CARRYING ON THE FIGHT IN MISSISSIPPI

Mickey Schwerner

James Chaney

Andrew Goodman

HEAR
Mrs. Fanny Chaney
Courageous Mother of James Chaney
At New Zion Baptist Church
2319 THIRD STREET
THURS., AUG. 27, 1964
7:30 P. M.
CORE

A flyer announcing a memorial for the three civil rights workers murdered by the Ku Klux Klan and buried in the earth dam of a cattle pond on June 21, 1964. On August 4, the bodies of Schwerner, Goodman, and Chaney were uncovered by the FBI. On the same day, President Johnson began the bombing of North Vietnam.

Freedom Schools conducted classes in literacy, history, and voter registration in rural towns all over Mississippi.

Congressman Don Edwards of California is greeted at the school in Ruleville.

155

Two of the many volunteers who met in the summer of 1964

A cafe in Ruleville

Saturday in Drew

Some of the negatives and prints on these pages—everything I photographed in Mississippi during July and August of 1964—were missing for twenty-four years. I had long ago become resigned to the fact that I would never see them again. Then, as I began assembling the material for this book, the Black Star Photo Agency moved from one Manhattan office to another, and the lost negatives, which had been stored there, were found. Because they were found, the pictures for this section on the Mississippi Summer could be printed.

But some of the negatives were not found, and as far as I know no prints were ever made from these rolls. The only thing that exists are the contact sheets once made from them, which were in the Black Star files. A copy negative was made from the contact sheets so that reproductions could appear in this book. The originals are forever lost, and some of the people pictured in them are lost also, long departed from the world that in their youths they struggled so to change.

Politics wasn't our only concern in Mississippi that summer. Sam Shirah met a summer volunteer from St. Paul and married her. I met Heidi Dole, a volunteer from Santa Barbara. We all piled into my Oldsmobile to visit the new Freedom House in Biloxi. Someone said the salt water would be good for our mosquito bites.

That fall I went to New York to get things from my parents' home and then drove back down south with a driveaway car, pulling a trailer and my motorcycle, not much used since I had left it behind in Chicago. With me was a veteran from Harlem, Bruce Gordon, one of the many new people filling the ranks of the movement. Somewhere in Virginia during a rainstorm, the windshield wipers stopped working, and we pulled into a garage while Bruce climbed up on the roof to repair them. As I searched the glove compartment for tools, I ran into a heavy metal lump wrapped inside a rag. Bruce was bringing something besides his convictions down to Mississippi; he was also bringing a gun.

I dropped him off at the office in Jackson and headed west toward New Orleans. Exhausted from driving all night, I pulled off the road with the used car I was driving, orange trailer in tow, and went to sleep. That night a hurricane passed over me. In the morning the car was covered with branches and tree limbs, and the road I had parked on was underwater. A farmer on a tractor came along and, probably feeling sorry for me in my ineptitude, attached a chain under my car and pulled me out.

I made the picture of Sam in New Orleans. He was living there. So were Peter de Lissovoy and Matt Heron and his family. John O'Neal and the Free Southern Theater were there also: I moved there too. The world of SNCC was no longer mine, and I had been inalterably changed by the experience. From then on I would try to create a new world. So would Sam, only he didn't live to write about it. He was murdered in Woodstock, New York, in 1980, shot with a rifle as he sat having breakfast with his wife and children. He was one of the finest people I ever knew.

Sam Shirah of Troy, Alabama, descendant of Confederate soldiers, SNCC field secretary, leader of the 1963 Postman's March that ended in Kilby State Prison, a fine guitar player and companion, murdered in Woodstock, NY in 1980

Bruce Gordon, a veteran, actor, and resident of Harlem and a SNCC field secretary, drove down with me from New York on his way back to Jackson, Mississippi. Here, somewhere in Virginia, he is trying to repair the windshield wipers on our used driveaway car.

Heidi Dole and Gwen Gillom

Volunteers in Leake County

Dona Richards in the COFO office

Howard Zinn

Robert Moses

Dave Dennis of CORE

The Waveland Conference
November 1964

Lester MacKinney

In November SNCC held a conference in Waveland on the coast of Mississippi. Sam and I got on my Triumph and rode over, probably to look for girls. At that time I would rather have done almost anything other than sit through a conference. The endless arguments were a special torture for me. A lot of whites were there, along with a lot of newcomers who had come down for the summer. (At the end of the conference, over eighty new people, including many whites, were added to the staff—more than had comprised the entire SNCC staff when I first joined.) I remember somebody thought his or her coat had been stolen. A great discussion ensued over the missing coat. Then Bob Moses, who as always had been sitting on the floor, got up to speak. What difference did it make if anyone had stolen anything? Material things did not matter anyway, he said. It was better not to have anything. He seemed annoyed with the whole discussion.

On November 6, the committee voted to reconstitute itself. The time was long past when SNCC had been a collection of student representatives from movements on southern campuses. The staff itself had become the organization, something much more forceful than any campus group. It is Forman who proposes the changes. Then he turns to the staff and asks for a leave of absence.

As in all eras of historic change, time during these years seems to have been compressed. Enormous changes have been packed into the four brief years between 1960 and the Waveland conference, and still more quantum changes lie ahead. During the four years Forman has worked to shape SNCC and the southern movement, he has also been hospitalized for bleeding ulcers. It is Bob Zellner who emotionally defends Jim's right to a rest. In two-and-a-half years SNCC will have become an all-black organization, and Forman, no longer executive secretary, will sit in on the meeting that expels Zellner, a man who has fought beside Forman from the earliest days.

I was no longer a member of the SNCC staff. Bob Fletcher, Cliff Vaughs, Doug Harris, and Tamio Wakayama were all making photographs of the movement. Black nationalism was steadily becoming more influential, and I could see that there was no future for a white inside SNCC, certainly not in any leadership role. I knew I would probably never see them again, and so I carefully made a picture of every person inside the room. In fact, twenty-five years did pass before I saw most of the SNCC people again.

Jean Wheeler Smith (standing) and Jack Minnis (far right)

Ralph Featherstone   *Courtland Cox*   *Phyllis Cunningham*   *Worth Long*

Ralph Featherstone, a New York City elementary school speech teacher who has come south to run the McComb Freedom School, known as "Feather" to his many friends. In 1967 he will be SNCC's program director and in 1970, with SNCC in virtual demise, he will be killed by a bomb that blows up his car. Ralph Featherstone is buried in Africa, "a brother from across the seas who came to rest in the soil of his ancestors."

Mendy Sampstein

Janet Jemmott (later Janet Moses)

Dorie Ladner

Jimmy Bolton

Bob Moses

Mary King

Julian Bond

Montgomery, March 7, 1965

The last pictures I made of the movement for which the negatives were lost and no enlargements ever made. (Above left) Forman, no longer in overalls, is on the phone. He and SNCC oppose the march to Montgomery. (Above center) The spot where Jefferson Davis stood to be inaugurated as president of the Confederacy, ironically marked by a Star of David. (Above right) Dr. King as he appeared in court in Montgomery; by this time he and Forman were barely speaking.

With the new year, state troopers in Alabama became more and more violent. In Marion, Alabama, they attacked news crews and killed a demonstrator, Jimmy Lee Jackson. Then, on February 18 in Selma, a march of three or four hundred people led by Hosea Williams of the SCLC and Lafayette Surney of SNCC was stopped by a sheriff's posse armed with guns and cattle prods. Many members of the posse were not even in uniform but wore business suits.

Three days later, on Sunday, February 21, 1965, Malcolm X was assassinated in New York City. John Lewis had met Malcolm X during a long trip to Africa with his friend Don Harris. Malcolm X had come to Selma, where he spoke with the youngsters who were the backbone of the movement. SNCC was the one civil rights group Malcolm X never directly attacked. He said they weren't civil rights, anyway, they were human rights. More and more, the intelligentsia in SNCC was identifying with liberation movements in Africa and seeing the movement in America as part of the struggle of Third World peoples.

On March 7, the local Selma movement was ready to continue the march that had been halted on February 18. The SNCC people in Atlanta flat out refused to be part of it. What was the point of leading people into the almost certain violence of the Alabama Highway Patrol and Jim Clark's posse? John Lewis, a native of Alabama, felt so personally committed to the Selma movement that he insisted on going, though as an individual and not as a representative of SNCC. Bob Mants also went. As it became apparent that the march would be a fait accompli even without SNCC's official support, more and more fieldworkers from Atlanta and from Jackson, Mississippi, went to join it. What follows is the WATS line report as the Atlanta office learned via telephone of the calamitous events that day.

The marchers, who were attacked and beaten on the Edmund Pettus Bridge in Selma, were in a sense carrying out the last march of the movement. For the Selma march was the last to truly grow out of an organized local movement. It was followed two weeks later by a five-day march from Selma to Montgomery called by Martin Luther King, for which people arrived from all over America. King's march to Montgomery was more dangerous than the March on Washington but in other ways not unlike it. Neither was the product of a local southern movement; both were called by national organizations and were staged primarily for their media effect. In fact, the alliance between SNCC, the most radical of the southern organizations, and the SCLC—an alliance that had survived since the early days in Atlanta when Forman had convinced King to give SNCC a few hundred dollars a month—had collapsed.

(Following pages) Reproduced here are the WATS line reports of March 7, 1965, as they came into the Atlanta office from Jackson and Selma. First, a call at 3:00 P.M. says that John Lewis and Robert Mants are leading the march, which SNCC has refused to join. Then Ruth Howard calls at 4:00 to say that four carloads of SNCC staff are leaving Jackson for Selma. Five minutes later, Cleve Sellers calls to say the same thing. Then Lafayette Surney calls from Selma and gives a minute-by-minute description of one of the most brutal police attacks of the civil rights movement as he watches it from a pay phone on the street corner. Half an hour later, a wounded John Lewis calls from Brown's Chapel. In Atlanta, dedicated office workers write it all down. Surney's last calls, made from Good Samaritan Hospital, describe broken arms, broken legs, gassings, and John Lewis in the emergency room with "a hole in his head" and possible concussion.

W.E.Scott calls Atlanta from Brown's Chapel in Selma.
John Lewis, Chairman of SNCC and Robert Mants, SNCC staff, and
Hosea Williams, SCLC staff, are leading the march. They are
in the process of organizing into companies and squads, with
company commanders and squad leaders.

Larry Fox:
The people are at the bridge over the Alabama River; they have
to walk double file. A group of state troopers, plus white
people, plus Sheriff Clark and his posse, plus Al Lingo
head of the state highway patrol are on the other side of the
bridge.

Leading the march are John Lewis, Robert Mants, and
Hosea Williams. behind them are about 50 Selma people, then
SNCC staff member, Wilson Brown, then 50 more Selma people
then SNCC staff member Jesse Harrison, 50 more Selma people
and SCLC staff member, Eugene Pritchett.

Other SNCC staff members -- Willie Emma Schoot, Frank
Soracco, John Luitkys, Chris Wylie and Annie Pearl Avery --
haven't arrived yet.

3:45 p.m. Larry Fox
SCLC staff members Addy Young, James Bevel, Hosea Williams,
Ben Clark and Harry Boyd are on the scene.

JACKSON, 4 pm Ruth Howard
Four carloads of SNCC staff people are planning to leave
Jackson for Selma.

SELMA 4 p.m. Lafayette Surney, street corner
About 2000-3000 people are marching. Mr. Turner of Marion is
also leading. They are on the bridge now.

If the police stop the people, they will wait until they
are tear-gassed to leave.

This morning, John Lewis read a three-minute statement to
the press about why they were marching. SCLC's Andy Young told
Dr. King wasn't coming: because after he heard that Wallace
had given the State Troopers all power to stop the march, he
decided to work on getting as much Northern support as possible.
A minister from SCLC in Selma vowed they would bring every
minister from all over the country in to town.

JACKSON, 4:05 p.m. Cleveland Sellers
Four carloads of SNCC staff are leaving.

SELMA 4:06 p.m. Surney
Two carloads of possemen just went to the bridge. The police
are making local whites get indoors.

SCLC's Fauntleroy is in Washington DC talking to Congress-
men. A lot of churches in New York City which were contacted
earlier by SCLC are calling in. Radio stations are calling in
by direct lines.

SNCC's Annie Pearl Avery was just arrested--don't know
what for. She just passed by in a police car. Two local white
guys were also arrested.

Three doctors and six-seven nurses from the Medical Committee for Human Rights, also three ambulances are there.
4:15 p.m. State Troopers are throwing tear gas on them. A
few are running back. A few are being blinded by tear gas.
Somebody got hurt--don't know who.
4:15 p.m. They're beating them and throwing tear gas at them.
4:16 p.m. Police are beating people on the streets. Oh, man,
they're just picking them up and putting them in ambulances.
People are getting hurt pretty bad.
There were two people on the ground in pretty bad shape.
I'm going to leave in a few minutes--people are running back
this way.
4:17 p.m. Ambulances are going by with their sirens going.
People are running, crying, telling what's happening.

(continued)

Lafayette Surney, street, corner, continued:
4:18 p.m. Police are pushing people into alleys. I don't
know why. People are screaming, hollering.
        They're bringing on more ambulances. People are
running, hollering, crying.
4:20 p.m. People are running.
4:22 p.m. Police got somebody else; it's hard to tell who-
looks like they're taking them to the hospital.
        Three more ambulances went by. The ambulances are
picking them up off the ground. There goes another one. Two
more. There go three of them.
4:23 p.m. They're carrying people by.
4:25 p.m. It looks pretty bad. They're carrying people
by, putting people in ambulances, private ambulances. People
are running.
        Here come the white hoodlums. I'm on the corner of one
of the main streets.
        A lady said they tried to kill her.
        People in the streets who were marching look like
they're going back to the churches.
4:26 p.m. They're going back to the church. I'm going
too. Should be there in about five minutes.

4:32 p.m. Brown's Chapel Church

James Austen
State troopers are outside the church throwing rocks.
John Lewis
People marched, 1500 to 2000 of them, marched down Highway
80, across the bridge. At the other side of the bridge were
200 State Troopers, 200 possemen, about 1000 white people.
The Major of the State Troopers made an announcement that
they should turn around. The people refused. They knelt to
the ground in a prayerful manner. Then the State Troopers
fired tear gas at them and began to beat them. I was hit in
the head.
        People went back to the church. There are about 2000-
3000 in the church. The posse is coming down to the church.
People on horseback are beating people with whips and ropes.
They are shooting tear gas.
        I've never seen anything like it in my life. They are
shooting gas, acid.
        One very odd lady I know has a broken arm.
Billy Bailey
I was across the bridge almost to the front of the line.
A number of people were beat by State Troopers. They started
walking toward us. When they started walking toward us, we
walked back. We kneeled and started to pray. Then they
started throwing gas. Then we just started running back.
4:40 p.m. Willie Emma Scott
We have a problem--the guys are not non-violent any more.
They're ready to fight. About two or three busloads of possemen are in front of the church beating people, throwing
tear gas, beating children and adults. They have about
twenty people on horseback. I don't know how many's been
carried to the hospital.
        John Lewis has a small hole in his head. I tried to do
something for it, but he wouldn't let me. They say Christo-
pher Wylie is in pretty bad condition. Another lady has her
arm broken in two or three places.
4:45 p.m. They didn't only throw tear gas at the people,
but also sprayed it on them so their clothes are full of it.
The church is full of tear gas.

Atlanta 5:05 p.m. Ralph Featherstone, Ivanhoe Donaldson,
Courtland Cox, and RoybShields left here by plane for Selma.

Selma 5:14 p.m. Good Samaritan Hospital
Lafayette Surney
People had their legs, arms broke. Fractures of legs, arms.
Tear gas--that's the baddest thing. The ambulance made

                        (continued)

Lafayette Surney, Good Samaritan Hospital, continued:

several trips. They trampled over people with horses.
The people at the church started throwing bricks ath the
State Troopers.

5:30 p.m.   Brown's Chapel Church
Larry Fox
The church is surrounded by possemen on horseback with
tear gas.
        People are in the hospital. Doctors are next door to
the church.
5:34 p.m. Wilson Brown
The church is surrounded by possemen, State Troopers, and
Jim Clark. They have Sylvan Street (the street the church
is on) blocked off from one end to the other.so people
can't get in or out of the church. They are forcing people
to go back into their homes, beating them with billy sticks.

6 p.m. Good Samaritan Hospital Nurse Thomas
So far there have been no reports of people having been shot,

6:15 p.m. Brown's Chapel Larry Fox
There is a rumor that if the people don't leave the church,
it will be raided by State Troopers. This came through a
funeral home.
        Tear gas was shot into a house down the street by State
Troopers.

6:20 pm Good Samaritan Hospital Worth Long
John Lewis is in the hospital with a possible skull fracture.

6:21 p.m. The people have just come back from the airport.
There was no one there. It was hard getting there, and hard
getting back, and it will probably harder to get out again.

6:30 p.m. State Troopers and possemen have left.

ATLANTA 7 p.m.
James Forman called Dr. Martin Luther King to discuss the
situation in Selma. Dr. King's secretary said that Dr. King
was busy preparing a statement on Selma and could not be
disturbed. Forman left word asking that Dr. King return his
call.

SELMA 7:05 p.m. Good Samaritan Hospital
Lafayette Surney
John Lewis is still in the emergency room and will have to
stay over night. There is the possibility of a concussion.
I just finished talking to Police Commissioner Baker. He
said that Saate Troopers took over and just took it out of
their hands.

8:30 p.m. Brown's Chapel Church
Willie Emma Scott
People are gathering at the church for a mass meeting.
John Lewis is still in the hospital.

Note: All times given are Eastern Standard Time (Atlanta
time). Alabama time is one hour behind.

The night after King's march passed through Lowndes County, Alabama, Viola Liuzzo, a Detroit mother of five children, was shot to death by the Klan while she was driving in her car with a young black companion. Her passenger, Leroy Moton, miraculously survived by playing dead. When twenty-one-year-old Collie Leroy Wilkins was charged with Liuzzo's murder, the Klan's chief counsel defended him. Following are excerpts from his speech.

> And this white woman who got killed? White woman? Where's that N.A.A.C.P. card? I thought I'd never see the day when Communists and niggers and white niggers and Jews were flying under the banner of the United Nations flag, not the American flag we fought for. . . . I'm proud to be a white man and I'm proud that I stand up on my feet for white supremacy. Not black supremacy, not the mixing and the mongrelization of races, . . . not the Zionists that run that bunch of niggers. The white people are not gonna run before them. And when white people join up to 'em they become white niggers. . . . Do you know those big black niggers were driven by the woman, sitting in the back seat? Niggers! One white woman and these niggers. Right there. Riding right through your county.

Wilkins was not convicted of the murder. Eventually the federal government retried him for violating Mrs. Liuzzo's civil rights. With Wilkins in the car when he chased down Leroy Moton and Viola Liuzzo had been four other Klan members, including Gary Rowe, who was at the time a regular paid informant for the FBI. Rowe testified against his fellow Klansmen at the trial, emerging from six years of undercover federal employment. Under federal law, Collie Wilkins was convicted of violating Mrs. Liuzzo's civil rights and sentenced to ten years in prison.

Gary Rowe's simultaneous roles as member of the KKK and informant for the FBI placed him in the thick of some of the most important unexplained events of those times. Rowe joined the Klan in 1958 at the request of the FBI. He was present at the 1961 attack on the Freedom Riders in Birmingham and was photographed standing next to Klan member Robert Chamblis as they both beat the riders. He had reported to the FBI that the attack was planned. Taylor Branch claims that the Birmingham FBI office told the Washington bureau about the planned Klan attack five different times, beginning nine days before it happened. Did some people in our government also know beforehand that a bomb was going to be placed at the Sixteenth Street Baptist Church? No known evidence exists that Rowe knew of the plot or was there, but it was Robert Chamblis who was convicted in 1977 by the federal government of violating the young girls' civil rights by blowing them up with a bomb.

How much was Gary Rowe paid? What other Klan activities did he inform the FBI about? We may never know. At the Liuzzo trial, where Rowe revealed his role as Klan informant for the FBI, his testimony was greatly restricted by his employers, and he was not allowed to give testimony on his prior relationship with the Klan.

It was always SNCC's policy to go into the most dangerous areas; if changes could be brought about there, they would follow elsewhere. After participating in a march it hoped to avoid, SNCC decided to move into Lowndes County, led by the twenty-four-year-old Stokely Carmichael and by Cleve Sellers of North Carolina. Lowndes County was as deep into the Black Belt as one could go. The county was mostly black, but no blacks voted. Jonathan Daniels, a New Hampshire

Willie Ricks was one of SNCC's great stump speakers, capable of getting great emotional responses from a crowd. During the Meredith March in Mississippi, where King and Stokely Carmichael marched side by side, it was Ricks who first unleashed the "Black Power" cry. Here he speaks in Atlanta.

minister who had come down for the march to Montgomery and stayed to work in Lowndes County, was with them. Daniels was among a group of people arrested in the small town of Fort Deposit and forced out of the jail at night. Shot point-blank with a shotgun, he died at the feet of Gloria House, a new SNCC worker from Berkeley.

There was more carnage to come. On January 4, 1966, five years after the movement had begun with nonviolent sit-ins, twenty-two-year-old Sammy Younge, a Navy veteran, Tuskegee student, and SNCC voter registration worker, was murdered in Tuskegee, Alabama. He was trying to use the restroom in a gas station when he was shot in the head. The awful murder of this popular young man was devastating to SNCC. (Forman later published a book about him, entitled *Sammy Younge, Jr.: The First Black College Student to Die in the Black Liberation Movement*.)

On the heels of Sammy Younge's murder, SNCC issued its first statement against the war in Vietnam. Nine years before the war finally ended—long before most other organizations—SNCC publicly attacked the war policy of the Democrats and the Johnson administration. Soon afterward Dottie Miller, now Dottie Zellner, attended the staff meeting in Atlanta. She had been to every one since the fall of 1961. "I remember the SNCC meeting with unbearable clouds of smoke. I was sitting there with a baby, six months old, at one o'clock in the morning. Miss Baker was sitting at the far edges wearing her smoke mask which she always did. The smoke was practically impenetrable. And I remember Cleve Sellers asked to hold the baby. This tall thin very handsome black guy was holding this baby who of course was coughing her head off."

The consensus of the meeting was that Julian Bond, who had just been elected to the Georgia State House of Representatives with 82 percent of the vote in his district, should not disavow SNCC's statement against the war. When he did support the antiwar stand, the Georgia legislature refused to seat him. (After Bond had fought for his rights in court for two years, the Supreme Court finally supported him and ordered that he be seated.) The attacks on Bond came not primarily from the right, but from the liberals and the left. Vice President Humphrey called Bond's declarations "obnoxious," while the *New York Times* called him a "misguided young man" and suggested that the ballot box would be the proper place to "punish" him.

If only this nation had had the courage and the will to follow our Julian Bonds. The nine years of bloody war that followed put a drain on our economy from which we have not yet recovered and may never recover. Fifty thousand Americans and over one million Vietnamese died there—and for what?

The "beloved community" that had represented the early civil rights movement had indeed come apart. That it lasted as long as it did is all the more remarkable when we become aware of the tensions beneath its surface.

In May 1966, James Meredith, the veteran who had integrated the University of Mississippi in the fall of 1962, was shot and wounded as he made a one-person march through Mississippi. SNCC and the SCLC agreed to continue the march, and Stokely Carmichael, SNCC's new chairman, and Martin Luther King ended up walking across Mississippi together. In a Delta town, Willie Ricks, a powerful stump speaker, unveiled SNCC's new slogan: Black Power. Ricks said the local people really liked it. To the press it was like a red flag in front of a bull. As the movement that SNCC represented was ebbing, the militancy of its rhetoric increased. Too many people had died. There were few left to enter the ranks and say they would be nonviolent. What was left of SNCC's financial support, already slowed by the group's antiwar stand, now came to a grinding halt.

Peg Leg Bates, Kerhonkson, N.Y.
December 1966

On Route 209 in the Catskills, near my present home, a billboard for Peg Leg Bates still stands, probably not painted since the fateful conference held there a generation ago.

On May 8, 1966, SNCC met at Kingston Springs near Nashville. John Lewis was reelected chairman, but then Worth Long, a close friend of SNCC, came into the late-night meeting, claiming that some people had not been represented in the vote and demanding that it be held again. SNCC meetings could be very informal, so although Worth Long was not even a member of the group at that time, Lewis acquiesced and the vote was held again. This time Lewis was replaced by twenty-four-year-old Stokely Carmichael. Lewis, by his own admission, was stunned. "But he's not even a southerner," he is reported to have said.

A generation later, I sat with Congressman Lewis in his Washington office as he recalled that day. He said he had recovered quickly from what at the time was a devastating rejection. But it had been a momentous event, and even across that great gulf of time, I sensed the pain the veteran activist from Alabama had felt. "Remember what they used to say?" The closed-circuit television that is always running in every congressman's office was calling Lewis to vote. "I was married to the movement. It was my whole life."

Soon after being voted out as chairman, John left the SNCC staff. He did not go quietly. In July the *Los Angeles Times* published a story on John and quoted him as saying that Forman, who had been replaced as executive secretary by twenty-three-year-old Ruby Doris Robinson (Smith), was really the most powerful person in SNCC. "Most Negroes," Lewis said, "will never identify with black nationalists and other black reactionaries who talk loud and use cutting words like 'Black Power,' but also never engaged in confrontations to bring about change." He further warned that if the nonviolent movement failed to win support for housing and jobs, it would degenerate. Around that same time, President Lyndon Johnson ended a television address on voting rights by invoking the movement's slogan, "We shall overcome." Andy Young claims that as Dr. King watched the speech, King cried. I watched that speech also and, in the terminology of the times, I "wanted to puke." I was outraged that the target of the antiwar movement would co-opt the slogan of the civil rights movement.

From December 1 to December 8, 1966, a staff retreat was called in Kerhonkson in the Catskill Mountains of New York State. The meeting has come to be known as Peg Leg Bates after the name of the black entertainer at whose resort it was held. SNCC meetings could be long and contentious. Chuck McDew said that meetings went on "for ever and for ever and for ever." This one went on for seven days and spelled the end of the band of interracial brotherhood and sisterhood born in the flames of the Freedom Rides. Recalling those years today, Julian Bond feels that SNCC developed in stages, metamorphosing every six months as new people came into the organization, adding to those who were still there and replacing others who had left, each phase carrying SNCC and the movement forward.

At Peg Leg Bates, after an extremely contentious meeting, a new butterfly emerged from a cocoon that had been a long time in forming. The meeting was so chaotic that it was not completely clear to many people who were present what actually had been decided there. (Twenty-five years later, it is still not completely clear.) Approximately one hundred staff members were present at the conference. At two o'clock one morning, when many of the staff had gone off to go to sleep, SNCC passed a resolution to exclude whites. Nineteen voted for the resolution, eighteen voted against it, and twenty-four people abstained, including all the white people present. This was a very SNCC-like gesture; Bob Zellner later said it was "not proper" for whites to use their own votes to stay in the organization. To this day, many SNCC veterans think that the whites were not thrown out but instead were directed to work in the white community.

There had always been present in SNCC the idea that only black people could liberate black people. Also always present was the concept of developing indigenous black leadership and always presenting blacks in leadership positions. In the words of Bob Zellner, "Our leaders were black people, pure and simple." The vote at Peg Leg Bates brought to the fore the influences of African nationalism and the writings of the Algerian Frantz Fanon and of Malcolm X.

The discussion of this issue that follows took place in Atlanta in May 1967, six months after Peg Leg Bates. The occasion was not a meeting of the full Coordinating Committee but of the smaller Central Committee, and one of the arguments going on was that this smaller group could not undo what had been decided previously by the full committee. It was not even clear to everyone in the room what actually *had* been decided at Peg Leg Bates. Forman said that three votes were taken and that in one of them it was decided that whites could not have a vote in SNCC. By this time Stokely Carmichael had been replaced as chairman by Rapp Brown. Forman was no longer executive secretary but was in charge of international affairs. Forman was, in fact, the only person in the room whose involvement went back to the beginning of SNCC. Julian Bond was gone. Bob Moses had gone to Canada to avoid the draft. He had also changed his name to Parris, his mother's name, and he had told Mendy Sampstein, with whom he had worked for years, that Mendy was the last white person he would ever talk to.

There is great pathos in this scene, as the last white field secretary appears before the Central Committee and demands the right for himself and his wife, Dottie, to keep working for SNCC. The parents of two children, the Zellners are ready to go organize within the white community, but they insist that they must have a vote within SNCC like everyone else. Bob Zellner's involvement with SNCC predates that of everyone in the room with the exception of James Forman. His credentials as an activist are impeccable. He has repeatedly risked his life for the movement. Forman himself is married at the time to Dinky Romilly, a white, and has two children by her. Zellner's wife Dottie is one of Forman's closest friends. Although it is Zellner who stands before the committee, in fact Dottie has written the proposal that the committee considers.

The tension in the rooms cries out from the page, as a number of those present refuse categorically to make a decision based on race. Zellner is asked to wait outside the room during most of the discussion. Finally he is asked in and told that because he insists on a vote, he cannot work for SNCC. Despite the rejection, Zellner announces that he will remain silent about the decision, so that what has been done to him cannot be used against SNCC in the press. Like a loyal Bolshevik, he goes before the firing squad praising the revolution. In a final moment he asks for a copy of the proceedings, so that Dottie can see how he stood up for himself. In fact his appearance is an act of great personal bravery, based on principle—something that Forman recognizes and agonizes over. Dottie later called SNCC's decision "the worst thing that had ever happened to me in my life."

Five years had passed since I first photographed SNCC in Albany, Georgia. Most people were no longer paying much attention to SNCC. The Black Panther party of Oakland, California, had stepped onto center stage. With their image of the armed and militant black, the Black Panthers attracted the attention of the world and also of the police, who proceeded to murder them, hound them, and drive them into exile. Some Panthers were targeted for extinction by the FBI. In August 1967, three months after the vote that expelled Zellner from SNCC, J. Edgar Hoover ordered the FBI to "disrupt, misdirect, discredit, or otherwise neutralize" black nationalist "hate-type" organizations. One of the groups selected was SNCC.

Simultaneously, another great storm was sweeping across America. In October 1967, on the steps of the Pentagon, I was knocked unconscious. It took six stitches to close the wound in my scalp. This was a worse injury than anything I had experienced at the hands of southern police. I have never forgotten that the club was wielded not by a southern racist but by a United States marshall, a paid employee of the federal government. Seven hundred people were arrested that night at the Pentagon; I was the fourth. A new and powerful movement was upon the land, fighting to stop a war that would continue for another eight bloody years.

With the rise of the antiwar movement, SNCC passed from the national consciousness and into history. Many individuals from SNCC stepped directly into the struggle against the war. Courtland Cox sat on Bertrand Russell's war crimes tribunal in Stockholm. Julian Bond's long struggle to be seated in the Georgia State House made national news. Diane Nash visited Hanoi. John Lewis spoke out against the war in the streets of Harlem. In 1968 police in Orangeburg, South Carolina, shot four black college students to death, wounded Cleve Sellers, and then indicted him for inciting a riot. Sellers spent eight months in a federal prison for refusing the draft.

The jury is still out on what has been ubiquitously labeled the Sixties, a decade born among these people, mostly young black activists from the South. May this work be a lasting trophy to the people pictured in it, my ballot on the scales of history.

James Forman and the Zellners, photographed in Danville in 1963

Reproduced on the following pages are excerpts from the SNCC Central Committee meeting notes of May 1967 in Atlanta. Participants include Bill Hall (Winkie), Fay Bellamy, John Wilson, Stanley Wise, Bob Zellner, Rapp Brown, George Ware, and James Forman. The original transcription of this discussion, which was recorded by Fay Bellamy and Evelyn Marshall, covers twenty-five pages and ends with the words "tape ran out." The many omissions made here are marked by asterisks.

Ethel: Didn't we finalize at this staff meeting the staff cate-
                gories -- voting and non-voting? We made a decision that
white people would no longer have a note in the policy making decisions .

Rapp: The vote said that they could no longer be members of
                the decision making body. We have records of the Peg Leg
Bates decisions. Forman, can you recall the votes.

Forman: Yes, there were three votes. Sunday night, no white
                people. The final vote was that we have whites who work
for the organization but that they would not take place in policy making
decisions of the organization. That if the Coordinating Committee meets,
they will not vote.

Winkie: It was my understanding that white folks would no longer
                be a part of the organization.

Bob Fletcher: My understanding was that they would no longer be a part
                of the Coordinating Committee and I just don't think we
should start this whole thing over again.

Fay: One thing that was added was white people would be worked
                with on a contractual basis.
                                              / was
John Wilson: What I thought was passed that white folks would no longer
                have a part in the organization and the staff was supposed
to deal with that situation.

Stanley: I would like to ask for a point of procedure and my point
                is we should not get bogged down in any technicality.
I just feel that if this body wills or wishes to changes its decision
or modify, then we can do it. We are the elected representatives of this
organization and I would just like to feel that we should get to the de-
tails of the things that you plan and then that we make a decision based
on that. I don't think that we should make a decision on what we voted
for at the last Central Committee meeting. I am now a leader in this
organization chosen by the people.

Fay: This body did not make that decision, number one. And I
                don't think this body can change that decision. I would
fight against that the rest of the god-damn day because we do not have
that right. We have the right to make decisions in the absense of the
group not to change the decisions that the Coordinating Committee has already made.

                        ★   ★   ★

Rapp:

                It has been moved and seconded that at this point of
the discussion that Bob Zellner be asked to leave the room because we
are getting ready to discuss his status.

Bob: I would just like to make a statement on the proposal.

Fay: One reason I think that Bob should leave the room is
                most of us here know Bob and some of us know him quite
well and I think that basically a lot of us had disagreements about how
the vote went down at Peg Leg Bates and that we have to get over that.

Now there is a way to do a thing and a way not to do a thing and I
think it would be better for Bob, for discussion and for us if he were
to leave the room.

    Rapp: Bob would you like to make your statement before de-
                parting.

Bob: Yes, I would. I don't have any prepared statement or any-
        thing. I just want to say something about ... First of
all, I'll start with an analysis. That is I belong to a predominantly
white organization and they took the move that we took at Peg Leg Bates
to limit the members categorically to black people. I was the first
white person to fight against it as other people did and secondly, I
respect any black people involved who will stand up for their rights.

In the same position, I would expect anybody to respect me for standing
up for my rights on a matter of principle. We don't have to go into
the history of my relationship but I feel, and have always felt, that
SNCC was as much a part of me as anybody else and that I was SNCC and
I will always be SNCC. To me, there is one very strong principle involved. Sncc has never required of anybody ... What I am saying is
that if anyone should take what happened at one meeting to be for all
times, there is something wrong with the democratic processes in this organization. And if in fact, there are principles involved, then we
should continue to fight for the type of relationship that we feel is
desirable.

My feeling is on my staff relationship is I have always considered myself as a SNCC field secretary and I will always consider myself a SNCC
field secretary and will always act like one but I have to take the
position that unless I, I'm not speaking for anybody else now, am accepted as a SNCC staff member as anyone else, then I can't consider myself a
staff member. It's either all or nothing. I will not accept any sort
of restrictions or special categories because of race. We do not expect other people to do that in this country and I will not accept it for
myself. So I just leave with that statement. It is a statement of
principle and if we are going to work together, then we will work together.
Otherwise, we will continue but I can't consider myself a staff member
in any sense.

Winkie: I would like to know if you would be willing to have your
          status maintained and to be excluded from meetings.

Zellner: I think this is a matter we will have to take up later
          on. My decision is that is that I am either a SNCC staff
member or I'm not.

                (Zellner leaves the room.)

Rapp: The chair opens for discussion in light of the decisions
        we have made, in the light of the type of organization
we want, in the light of our hope to become a revolutionary force and also in the light of the fact that this may occur again and again.-

Winkie: I have viewed these things ... I hope that ... The reason
          is that we have to raise questions about the relation-
ship. In reference to the Algerian war, we said that they understood the

And so, I want to know if he sees himself in that revolutionary sense.
I don't think that the exclusion should be based upon his race, it should
be based upon his idenitification. Will he identify with us? And that
as a technician that he could be used.

                ★   ★   ★

George Ware: First of all, I would like to say that I agree with
               Bob Zellner in terms of the either / or situation. I
think the question is that if you are trying to resolve what is a very
touchy problem, the discussion should be around whether or not he is on
staff or off staff. I think that the basis of that discussion comes
from the fact that, like I agree emphatically with the decision at Peg
Leg Bates, the only thing I disagreed with this was the way that it was
carried out. I thought it was very sloppy and kind of barbaric but I
agree that white people should not play decision making roles in SNCC.
That whites should not be on SNCC staff and I think that based on that
decision, which I agreed with, or even if I didn't agree with it; I
would have to equate him not coming on SNCC staff. I would support
his proposal and I think that if there is anything that SNCC can do to
bolster out or to help that activity, that they should do it and that
is terms of any resources we might have or anything else.

★ ★ ★

Fay: I just think that it is very unfair of Bob Zellner, who I
think is a little more politically aware than myself, you know,
to bring that emotionalism into this room. He brought it in as
an emotional thing, as a self thing and as a friendship thing.

Now the cat should be aware that....I don't really think there is
any out and out racist sitting at the table here....but he should
understand, having had the connection with SNCC in the past, since
our inception practically, of the feelings and the rhetoric and
why those feelings and rehetoric now exist.

He should also be aware, and I think he is but refuses to admit it,
that there is a need for BLACK organization in this country. In
appearance, if nothing else. It makes all the difference in the
world to this organization and how we function in the community,
especially given the rhetoric that we have taken up these last
couple of years, to have even one white person sitting on the
Coordinating Committee.

Now it shouldn't make any difference, but it does.

★ ★ ★

Stanley: I think it is really unfortunate that we voted that
Bob should not be here, because I think this is a problem that
we have to confront and have to deal with. As the body has stated,
that as administrators, we are to carry out its positions and to
say things that they want us to articulate. I think that is an
injustice, but I tend to agree somewhat with Fay. Ithink that out
of what we have done over the past year and the past years, we have
evolved to the point that some black people in this country feel
somewhat safe at expressing themselves, at moving and doing things.
I think I heard it best put by Floyd McKissick when he said that,
some black people now strut upon the stage, and that is an important
thing to note.

Any policy, given the nature of the racism that we suffer in this
country, that the policies concerning black people and the projec-
tion has to come from black people. It has to come out of our
communities.

I think that it is unfortunate that a great deal of emotionalism
is involved and I know it is involved on both sides, and that Bob
cannot understand that. Black people must make these decisions.
I see at some future date, black and white people coming together.
I personally am willing to live with him being on our staff in a
nonvoting capacity. But I do think that the main thrust of the
organization and the main impetus at this moment, at this particular
date in our history, that we must determine for ourselves....I take
a great deal of impetus, I think, from Frederick Douglas when he
said, "that he that would be free must strike the first blow".

It is absolutely crucial that we strike the first blow. If Bob
does not wish to be, as he terms it, second-class, but as Fay said,
understanding that there is no racism involved...if he is not willing
to do that, then I see no alternative that this group has but to say
that he is fired.

I think to do anything else would be skirting the issue. That is
if we believe firmly in our position. I think that this is something
that we have to resolve, one way or the other.

Forman: I think that we are confusing some things. Bob is my best
friend.

?:   You said that about Fay the other day.

Forman: That is right goddamit. I have two best friends. The
point is that the issue is not the emotionalism involved, because
I know that I were he, I would be emotional too. If I had put in
that much energy in helping to build this organization on which
people are now operating, I would be very emotional about it. I
think we have to understand that.

* * *

Johnny: I find myself in a very pulling situation, as far as my
emotions are concerned. I just have a basic principal that I try
to keep. I don't have too many. One of them is that I don;'t
believe in systematic racism. I just don't believe in it. I
think it always comes back to haunt people that perpetuates it.

I realize,....I think I realize the situation that we are in. It
is my feeling that due to the situation that we are really in, that
we couldn't very well allow Bob to come on staff as a voting member.
I would just like to say that I think we should understand the
situation that we are in. I really do. I would just like to say
that if we have any sense of judgment, and any sense of responsibility
to the people that are involved in the organization at the present
time, that before we make decisions like this ever again, that we
should really take heed to know what we are doing.

I know the cat man. I've known the cat for a long time and have
been to some of the places where he was working and I just have a
hell of a lot of respect for him. I would never go against him as
far as putting him out of the organization because of his color.

* * *

Winky: There are still many of us in the organization who identify
with white people, and because we do, we have tremendous problems
of separating from them. We have to rise above the personal friendship level and as a group must strive to be objective as much as
possible.

There may come a time when we will pick up arms. I would like to
make a motion Mr. Chairman, but before I do, I would like to preamble
it with the fact that Ruby Doris, has to some extent, has give us
some direction, in terms of the letter she sent to Charlotte Carter.

She said that obviously the basis for determining memberships on
the Coordinating Committee was that, "Although you will remain a
part of the organization and a member of the staff, you will not
be considered a member of the Coordinating Committee. I think that
I see three main divisions in SNCC. There is what she has defined
as a member of staff. It is obvious that (couldn't hear this
part).

Forman: I consider that a personal insult.

Rap: You can address yourself to that in a response.

Forman: He doesn't know what the fuck is going to happen.
         Flip-Flop motherfucker.

* * *

(Bob Zellner is back in the meeting)

Rap: I think you (Bob) made it clear that our relationship would
not be severed and the only thing that is being cut is your privi-
leges as a staff member.

Bob: I just want to say that I went along with the decision at
Peg Leg Bates, mainly because I didn't know what/do, but I just
couldn't operate like that.   to

I think it is a mistake, but that is among us. As far as the press
is concerned, I don't have anything to say to them about this. I
shall continue to operate. I would like for you to make a statement
to be shown to the coordinating committee.

* * *

Bob: I don't know about access to the tape, but I know Dottie would
like to know, at least what I SAId, so I w-ould like to receive
a copy of that part.

Rap: O.K. We will do that.

Trinity College
Hartford, Connecticut
April 1989

Epilogue

In April 1989, Jack Chatfield, a teacher in the history department of Trinity College in Hartford, Connecticut, and a SNCC veteran (he had worked in southwest Georgia and managed to get shot on his first day out in the field), organized a three-day symposium called "We Shall Not Be Moved," about the life and times of the Student Nonviolent Coordinating Committee, 1960 to 1966. Almost everyone came. I had not seen most of them for twenty-five years, and for me it was like falling into a dream. My love for that time and for those with whom I shared it had been so strong that, as the years went by, I think I forgot that they were real people. Now they all sat before me, at the end of an auditorium in Connecticut. They were there to leave a record for history, they were there to tell their story to a new generation, and they were there to see each other.

Martha Prescod Norman, who had been a nineteen-year-old girl from Detroit when I had timidly watched her helping black sharecroppers cross the street to the Greenwood courthouse, spoke of the history of which she was now an instructor. From the age of sixteen to twenty-one, she had grown up and married in the movement. Her son with Silas Norman of the Selma movement was about to enter Harvard.

Martha lashed out at the mistakes that had entered the history books. The student movement had been the vanguard, she said. Students had sensed the power and capacity for struggle in the Black Belt communities and had carried the movement there. Real change had been brought about by "the constant, widespread, relentless activism of southern black communities." The movement had ended segregation in the South. It had brought the franchise to many areas where blacks had been kept from voting for one hundred years. Martha Norman also expressed something felt by many SNCC veterans: namely, that there is a reason why Dr. King has so often been exhibited as a model to the American people. "King and the civil rights movement have become so interchangeable that many of the students that come into my class have no idea that there was a black student movement in the 1960s." Not only students, but no Americans are taught of the power that is theirs beyond the ballot box.

At the Trinity College conference in 1989: (Top, left to right) Michael Thelwell, Courtland Cox, Kwame Ture (the former Stokely Carmichael), Gloria House, Cleveland Sellers, Mendy Sampstein, Casey Hayden, and Jean Wheeler Smith. (Bottom, left to right) Julian Bond, Charles McDew, Diane Nash, Robert Zellner, Charles Sherrod, James Forman, Bernard Lafayette, and me.

Now they were mayors, Ph.D.'s, teachers, parents, authors, and revolutionaries, and whatever the politics and divisions of SNCC's closing years, the now middle-aged SNCC workers literally fell into each other's arms.

Mike Thelwell, the author and professor of Afro-American Studies at the University of Massachusetts, sat on the Black Power panel with Cleve Sellers and Courtland Cox. He virtually apologized to Casey Hayden, Mendy Sampstein, and Bob and Dottie Zellner, all of whom were in the room, for the vote at Peg Leg Bates, even though Thelwell had not been present there. Had more SNCC veterans been at the meeting, he felt, the vote would not have turned out the way it did. Thelwell had, on behalf of SNCC, always gone to whites to ask for help "out of the goodness of their hearts," an irony that was not lost on him. "We had no cards to play," is how he put it. Cleve Sellers said, "No longer were we just seeking the moral transformation of America. We had begun to change, to talk about the empowerment of black people." The call to Black Power, they explained, had been irresistible.

Thelwell spoke about the unfinished agenda of the black community, which was to organize in the ghettos of the great cities of the North. In 1966 he and Courtland Cox had written a Black Power paper on the subject, "from which I would quote if I had my glasses." Courtland read it for him.

> Negroes will in the next three decades control the heart of our great cities. These areas can become either concentration camps with a bitter and volatile population whose only power is the power to destroy, or organized and powerful communities able to make a constructive contribution to the total society. Without the power to control their lives and their communities, without effective political institutions through which to relate to the total society, these communities will exist in a constant state of insurrection. This is a choice the country will have to make.

I'm not sure the country ever really got the chance to make a choice. Black Power was portrayed by the press as simple racism, while SNCC's early antiwar stand branded its members "unpatriotic." They were, in fact, great patriots and believers in freedom in the highest sense of the word.

Casey Hayden added another sentiment when she wrote in the introduction to her friend Mary King's book: "I think we were the only Americans who will ever experience integration. We were the beloved community, harassed and happy, just like we'd died and gone to heaven and it was integrated there. We simply dropped race."

Almost thirty years separate the time when I first made photographs for SNCC and today. This book was begun by a boy and finished by a man. I made it for Sam Shirah, a boy I loved. And I made it for Ruby Doris Smith. I was so afraid of Ruby that I had to sneak up on her at the March on Washington just to make her photograph. A student activist in Atlanta in 1961, she was a Freedom Rider at a time when CORE thought the rides too dangerous to continue. She rode the integrated buses into Jackson even though she seldom spoke to whites. She never spoke to me. Ruby Doris gave seven years of her life to SNCC, and her jail time did not improve her health. She died of cancer in 1967. And I made the book for Jim Forman, who believed in me, apparently even more than I believed in myself, and for all those countless kids and for their children. I made it because I think SNCC, particularly in the early years, is a model for any group that wants to turn America into what it could be, but is not. I made it for us all.

The closed and boarded-up Mount Zion Baptist Church in Albany, Georgia, today. "I remember when people were standing by the windows, hanging from the trees, trying to get inside," said Charles Sherrod as I made the picture.

Sources

I have made use of many sources to fill in the parts of this story not covered by my personal experiences. As I struggled with a framework to present my photographs of SNCC, I realized that my memory of my life almost thirty years ago was not particularly good. SNCC had ceased to exist as an organization in the late 1960s, but for years I had heard that its files had survived. The main SNCC office had been in Atlanta, but there were also offices in Greenwood, Mississippi, and important "Friends of SNCC" offices in Chicago and New York. In fact, SNCC, an organization that grew out of the actions of college kids, had offices of various sizes all over the place and had left a substantial paper trail. There was a compulsion to write everything down, partly for legal reasons, as many SNCC activities and the frequent abuses of movement people later became cases in court.

James Forman, SNCC's guiding light, was a historian and often reminded people to record what he knew were historic events. People like Dottie Miller and Mary King, who worked in the Atlanta office, turned out reams of typed documents. Field offices were constantly issuing "press releases" that, in effect, were writing history on the spot. Discussions in the Atlanta office and in offices in the field were recorded by hand, as they took place, by some indefatigable worker. Later they were recorded by machine and then transcribed. Most of this material has survived. It is preserved in the SNCC archive at the Martin Luther King, Jr., Library in Atlanta and in the Social Action Collection at the State Historical Society of Wisconsin in Madison, and it is available on microfilm as the SNCC Papers in many libraries, including the Library of Congress. These documents and the information in them constitute the most important basis for the text of this book. Whenever possible, I have reproduced documents that can speak to us across the years. They have not changed at all. It is we who have changed.

Books

Branch, Taylor. *Parting the Waters: America in the King Years, 1954–1963.* New York: Simon and Schuster, 1988.

Bullard, Sara, and Julian Bond, eds. *Free at Last: A History of the Civil Rights Movement and Those Who Died in the Struggle.* Montgomery, Ala.: Civil Rights Education Project, The Southern Poverty Law Center, n.d.

Cagin, Seth, and Philip Dray. *We Are Not Afraid: The Murder of Goodman, Schwerner, and Chaney and the Civil Rights Campaign for Mississippi.* New York: Macmillan, 1988.

Carson, Clayborne. *In Struggle: SNCC and the Black Awakening of the 1960s.* Cambridge, Mass.: Harvard University Press, 1981.

Durr, Virginia Foster. *Outside the Magic Circle.* Tuscaloosa: University of Alabama Press, 1985.

Forman, James. *The Making of Black Revolutionaries.* 2d ed. Seattle, Wash.: Open Hand Publishing, 1985.

———. *Sammy Younge, Jr.: The First Black College Student to Die in the Black Liberation Movement.* New York: Grove Press, 1968.

Hansberry, Lorraine. *The Movement: Documentary of a Struggle for Equality.* New York: Simon and Schuster, 1964.

Hayden, Tom. *Reunion: A Memoir.* New York: Random House, 1988.

King, Mary. *Freedom Song: A Personal Story of the 1960s Civil Rights Movement.* New York: William Morrow, 1986.

Seeger, Pete, and Bob Reiser. *Everybody Says Freedom: A History of the Civil Rights Movement in Songs and Pictures.* New York: W. W. Norton, 1989.

Stoper, Emily. *The Student Nonviolent Coordinating Committee.* New York: Carlson Publishing, 1989.

Zinn, Howard. *SNCC: The New Abolitionists.* Boston: Beacon Press, 1964.

Articles
Interview with Sam Block. *Southern Exposure* 15, no. 2 (1988).
"Julian Bond: The Movement Then and Now." *Southern Exposure* 3, no. 4 (1976).
"Pictorial Summation of a Tragicomic Mistrial." *Life*, May 21, 1965, pp. 32–39.

Interviews
Ella Baker, "Mother of SNCC." Interview by Archie E. Allen, November 7, 1968, Harlem, N.Y.
Julian Bond. Interview by author, October 28, 1989, Washington, D.C.
John Lewis. Interview by Archie E. Allen, February 14, 1969, Atlanta, Ga.
John Lewis. Interview by author, October 27, 1989, Washington, D.C.
Charles Sherrod. Interview by author, December 25, 1989, Albany, Ga.
Bob Zellner. Phone interview by author, 1991.
Dorothy M. Zellner. Interview by author, November 30, 1989, New York, N.Y.

Tape Recordings
Malcolm X. "Grass Roots Speech," November 10, 1963, Detroit, Mich. Paul Winley Records, New York, N.Y.
The Trinity Conference, Trinity College, April 1989, Hartford, Conn. Also called "We Shall Not Be Moved: The Life and Times of the SNCC, 1960–66," the conference was tape-recorded and videotaped in its entirety. Especially helpful to me were statements by Gloria House, Bernard Lafayette, Charles McDew, Martha Prescod Norman, and Jean Wheeler Smith.

Records
Movement Soul: Live Recordings of Songs and Sayings from the Freedom Movement in the Deep South, recorded and edited by Alan Ribback. Distributed by ESP-DISK, New York, N.Y. ESP 1056.
Voices of the Civil Rights Movement: Black American Freedom Songs, 1960–1966, edited by Bernice Johnson Reagon. Smithsonian Institution, 1980.

"We Happy Few," 1955–1961

Because I did not witness the earliest events of the civil rights movement, I have relied more on other writers and on documents in this section of the book than in any other. I am particularly indebted to Taylor Branch for his great work, *Parting the Waters*, here and in many other areas of the book.

An almost equal debt goes to Archie E. Allen. Mr. Allen had the energy and foresight to tape-record and transcribe most of John Lewis's life, interviewing John, his family, and the people who knew him. The truly valuable thing about these transcripts, which cover hundreds of pages, is not just their extent but that they were made in 1968 and 1969, when the events being described were still close at hand.

We Are Not Afraid, by Seth Cagin and Philip Dray, has an extremely readable account of SNCC and the history that led to the martyrdom of Chaney, Schwerner, and Goodman. It was especially helpful in writing about the Nashville movement and the early days of SNCC.

In his autobiography, *Reunion*, Tom Hayden gives a great account of the early movement that he witnessed in Albany and Mississippi.

I interviewed Julian Bond in an office at the Washington Project for the Arts in October 1989, at which time he told me the story of the first Atlanta sit-ins with his usual charm and brilliance. Then I came upon the same story that Bond had told almost word for word to *Southern Exposure* magazine fourteen years earlier. I've used the story again here, but the discovery reaffirmed my desire to use as much material as possible that was made and recorded at the time the movement was going on, before the events had become a "story," etched in stone in some participant's mind, including my own.

Finally, Virginia Foster Durr's *Outside the Magic Circle* has wonderful descriptions of the early SNCC workers who came, unwashed and ragged, to her Alabama home for showers and food. In 1963 I became one of them when Forman brought a bunch of us there for the only real meal I ever had in a white southerner's home. What I didn't realize at the time was that Virginia and Clifford Durr's daughter Ann was married to my cousin Walter Lyon, and as a consequence I was related to the people who helped Rosa Parks at that fateful moment in time.

SNCC press release, February 23, 1961, is from the author's collection.

"Letter from the Magnolia Jail" by Bob Moses, November 1, 1961. This letter has been widely quoted and reproduced in virtually every book on the civil rights movement that I have seen. It is often reproduced without the first and last lines. This complete version is from James Forman's *The Making of Black Revolutionaries*.

Letter from Tom Hayden to Al Haber, September 1961. This is the final paragraph of a two-page letter, a copy of which is in the SNCC archive in the King Library in Atlanta.

Cairo, Illinois, 1962
Documents

Letter from John Lewis to James Forman and Charles McDew, June 7, 1962. Original is in the King Library in Atlanta.

"Come Let Us Build a Better World Together," SNCC poster, in author's archive.

Albany, Georgia, August 1962

In 1968 Emily Stoper wrote a doctoral dissertation for Harvard on SNCC. In 1989 the dissertation was published with ten of her interviews (including ones with Jane Stembridge, Ella Baker, Fannie Lou Hamer, John Lewis, and others) by Carlson Publishing. Among other things, Stoper presents an analysis of SNCC's fundamental radicalism and the organization's view of itself.

Mississippi, September 1962
Documents

A copy of the letter from Jane Stembridge to Amzie Moore is in the SNCC archive at the King Library in Atlanta.

"Résumé of the Inquiry re: Robert Parris Moses, Conscientious Objector" is an excerpt from an eleven-page document in the author's archive.

Nashville, November 1962: The Annual SNCC Conference

Branch's account of the demonstrations that accompanied SNCC's Thanksgiving weekend conference has Sam Block getting sprayed in the face with a fire extinguisher wielded by an enraged Tic Toc owner. In fact, as I watched from a few feet away, Sam Block was stabbed with a pen as he stood at the entrance to the Tic Toc. I photographed him as he was led away in pain and pointing to the wound. If Block himself is the source of Branch's account, my guess is he was physically attacked often enough to mix up some of the events.

Mississippi, 1963
Documents

The March 27, 1963, press release from Greenwood, Mississippi, is in the author's archive.

Winona, Mississippi, June 9, 1963
Documents

The remarkable affidavit by Annell Ponder and Fannie Lou Hamer was taken down by Jean Levine, Wiley Brenton's secretary. It is excerpted from a copy of the eight-page document that is in the author's archive.

"Is He Protecting You?" SNCC poster, in author's archive.

Danville, Virginia, June 10, 1963

Like a handful of people before him, James Forman has both made history and recorded it. His *The Making of Black Revolutionaries*, first published in 1972 and reissued in 1985, remains a great record of the entire civil rights movement. I was influenced by Forman the man, whom I was around constantly in the movement, and I have been influenced by Forman the author and historian throughout this work. Although William Shakespeare wrote the words, "we happy few, we band of brothers," in *King Henry V* for the scene just before the battle of Agincourt, it was Forman, in his 1972 book *The Making of Black Revolutionaries*, who described SNCC as "a band of sisters and brothers in a circle of trust." "Band of brothers" and "a circle of trust" were among the many terms used at the time to describe the early movement. As we traveled together into Danville here, Forman's published account of those grim days was especially helpful.

Documents

"Danville, Virginia," SNCC pamphlet by Dottie M. Zellner, copy in author's archive.

Gadsden, Alabama, June 1963

Documents

My notes from the conversation with the Alabama Highway Patrol are in my archive. The document was written in a Gadsden motel room in 1963.

The Leesburg, Georgia, Stockade

Documents

The affidavit by thirteen-year-old Henrietta Fuller, describing conditions in the Leesburg stockade, is one of many that are in the author's collection. Some people were brought there in July, more during August. On August 31 an eleven-year-old girl was put into the stockade for two days.

Washington, D.C., August 28, 1963

In 1981 Clayborne Carson published *In Struggle*, one of the first serious historical works devoted to SNCC. His chapter on the March on Washington was particularly helpful here, as were Taylor Branch's and James Forman's books. All three authors discuss the censorship of John's speech in detail. Malcolm X's "Grass Roots" speech in which he blasts the march is available on tape and remains riveting listening today. Despite the repeated use on public radio of "We Shall Overcome" to celebrate anniversaries of the march, my distinct recollection is that singing of the song was prohibited at the march, and it was purposely left off the program.

Documents

The copy of John Lewis's speech is one of those given out at the march and is in the author's archive.

Birmingham, Alabama, September 12, 1963

Sometime during 1963, James Forman and Elizabeth Martinez (then Sutherland), an editor at Simon and Schuster, conceived of the idea of a photography book about the struggle in the South, the proceeds of which would go to SNCC. As I became more involved in the project I began to photograph specifically for the book. In 1964 Simon and Schuster published *The Movement: Documentary of a Struggle for Equality*, which sold for $1.95 in paperback. *The Movement*, which had a brief text by the then hospitalized and dying Lorraine Hansberry, went into five editions in this country and another in England, where Penguin published it as *A Matter of Colour*. Alan Rinzler replaced Elizabeth Sutherland as editor, and during one of my visits to the offices high above the Colossus at Rockefeller Center, Alan said, "See that typewriter in the next room?" He handed me a pile of my photographs and told me to sit down and write captions, all of which he published verbatim in the book. *The Movement*, which I named, was in a real sense an early version of this book. The captions written in 1963 remain one of the most accurate guides to when and where the pictures were made, and I have referred to them throughout this work.

Selma, October 7, 1963

The first book-length account of SNCC was published by Howard Zinn in 1964 as *SNCC: The New Abolitionists*. A teacher at Spellman College when the Atlanta movement began in 1960, Zinn was the first teacher on any Atlanta campus to come out in support of the students. His account of Freedom Day in Selma, which he witnessed, was a great help to me.

The recordings of Betty Mae Fikes and many others that Alan Ribback made, and that he issued under the name Moses Moon, were released as *Movement Soul*; they also appear on Bernice Johnson Reagon's three-record set, *Voices of the Civil Rights Movement*. These recordings, made during the height of the movement, are the best I have ever heard.

Mississippi, Fall 1963

Documents

"SNCC Wedding Stirs Arkansas Officials," from the Pine Bluff, Arkansas, office, is a typical SNCC press release, one of perhaps thousands that SNCC issued, almost none of which, according to Emily Stoper, were ever printed by the press. The original is in the author's archive. The hearts and flowers are the result of a romantic moment with my Apple computer.

Atlanta, November 22, 1963

Documents

"Discussion Comments on Kennedy's Death" reproduces the entire four-page document as it was transcribed by Mal Clissold. I am almost certain I was in the room during the discussion, and it is interesting that I did not speak up. Some of the participants are Nancy Stearns, James Forman, Jimmy Fox, Ivanhoe Donaldson, Mark Suckle, Dinky Romilly, Charlie Cobb, and Sam Shirah, whose name is misspelled. A copy of the transcription is in the King Library in Atlanta.

Hattiesburg, Mississippi, January 22, 1964

Howard Zinn was again helpful in recalling the events of this day. An article he wrote for *The Nation* is the source of the story about Oscar Chase.

Documents

"Dear Mom and Dad," February 12, 1964, is in the author's archive.

Atlanta, June 10, 1964: Staff Meeting

Documents

The staff meeting minutes of June 9–11 cover thirty-two pages. Three-and-a-half pages from June 10 are reproduced here in their entirety without any editing. A copy is in the author's archive.

Mississippi Summer, 1964

Documents

The Freedom News is in the author's archive and is one of many such newsletters that were published by Freedom Schools that summer.

"Died for Freedom," a CORE flyer, was given out at the Jackson church where James Chaney's mother spoke. Printed on pink, blue, and yellow sheets of paper, this flyer evokes as much emotion and sadness today as on the hot August night I received it. It is in the author's archive.

The account of Sam Shirah's death was given to me on the phone in 1991 by Bob Zellner, who had recruited Sam into SNCC twenty-eight years earlier. There is also a newspaper file on Sam's murder kept by the Woodstock, New York, public library.

Montgomery, March 7, 1965

Here I am once again in an area of the movement that I did not witness myself, so I am completely indebted to documents, interviews, conferences, and other authors for what I have been able to write. Much of what I learned about Gary Rowe came from a long and generous telephone conversation with Taylor Branch. Clayborne Carson has an excellent discussion of the disintegration of SNCC in his book. Lafayette Surney, the caller in the devastating WATS line report, was one of my closest friends within SNCC and for a while wanted to be a photographer. The report itself is a good example of the many telephone calls that were turned into typewritten documents, usually by the Atlanta office staff. I came across the Klan lawyer's rabidly racist speech when I purchased an old *Life* magazine from a street vendor in New York City. I am also indebted, in this chapter and throughout the book, to *Free at Last*, a publication of the Southern Poverty Law Center edited by Sara Bullard and Julian Bond. This powerful document, which is available for $2.75 (and at cost to classrooms) from the Civil Rights Education Project in Montgomery, tells the story of forty persons who gave their lives for the southern civil rights movement.

Documents

"Selma, Alabama, March 7, 1965, 3 P.M." is a WATS line report published in its entirety. The original is in the SNCC archive of the King Library in Atlanta.

Peg Leg Bates, Kerhonkson, N.Y., December 1966

Clayborne Carson gives a detailed account of the FBI's infiltration and disruption of Black Power groups. I am especially indebted to him for this information and for his account of the life and death of Ralph Featherstone.

Documents

Notes of the discussion in which the Zellners are expelled from SNCC are excerpted from a transcription that covers twenty-five pages and ends with the line, "The tape ran out." A copy of the complete transcript is in the SNCC archive of the King Library in Atlanta. Here it has been reproduced with the omissions clearly marked. It was almost as agonizing to edit this document as it was to relive the discussion. At the height of the argument Forman says, "I would like for this body to clarify what the status of the five remaining whites (is). Is Mary Varella [sic] white? Is she Brazilian? There are members of the Central Committee who talk about we can't split up families. . . . I move that we discuss and attempt to clarify the status of four other people who are considered white, and who we voted were staff, but had no vote." Maria Varela, who was present when my wife Nancy gave birth to our first child and later received a MacArthur Fellowship for setting up a weavers' co-op used mostly by Chicanos in northern New Mexico, would in fact remain on the SNCC staff until the organization ceased to exist.

"SNCC report, July 29, 1966" is taken from a *Los Angeles Times* story by Atlanta correspondent Jack Nelson. This report repeated, in two long pages, the entire interview between Lewis and Nelson. It is extremely damning either to SNCC or to Lewis, depending on who one agrees with. Lewis denounces the Black Power movement and argues that support for it within SNCC is "thin." Why was it issued as a report by SNCC? Probably either to show Lewis's "betrayal" or because some people within SNCC agreed with what Lewis was saying. It also presents Lewis not as the "physically brave figurehead," but as an extremely political person fighting for his intellectual and political beliefs. A copy of the original is in the author's archive.

Trinity College, Hartford, Connecticut, April 1989: Epilogue

I owe a double debt to Jack Chatfield, history teacher at Trinity College in Hartford, Connecticut. He organized the April 1989 conference on SNCC and, when it was over, sent me a complete set of recordings of the conference. Many of the people whom I had known as staff members and organizers in their youth were, in their maturity, sophisticated and enthralling speakers. In a way this book began where it ends, for listening to Mike Thelwell, Martha Norman, Jean Wheeler Smith, Bernard Lafayette, Chuck McDew, Cleve Sellers, Diane Nash, and all the rest made me want to go home and make this book. Now, three years later, I am done. It was more fun the first time.

Acknowledgments

I am deeply indebted to many people who have helped me with this book. My greatest thanks and a fond embrace go to my wife, fellow filmmaker, and partner in virtually all of my work, Nancy Lyon. Nancy encouraged me to go to the Trinity conference and to do the book from the beginning. We worked together in the King Library and went through thousands of documents. She traveled with me to Albany to see Charles Sherrod and to Jackson and the Mississippi Delta. She went over all the original layouts with me and typed the manuscript and captions over and over again. Her only reward has been the creation of a work that does homage to a group of people whom she believed in.

Many of the prints reproduced here came from the Magnum Photos Archive in New York, where the negatives have been preserved for a generation. I don't think it would have been possible to assemble the selection made here were it not for the help from Magnum. When no funds were available to make new prints, Doug Kuntz, working in the darkroom of the *East Hampton Star*, made hundreds for nothing. Lupe Alvarez and Vince Cianni also helped with the prints. Diane Ware, the archivist at the King Library in Atlanta, was very gracious and made it possible for Nancy and me to search through the SNCC archive there. Her assistant, Dorothy Veasey, made us over 500 photocopies. I am indebted to John Lewis, Dottie Miller Zellner, Charles Sherrod, Bob Zellner, June Johnson, Ruth Howard Chambers, Jack Chatfield, Dave Garrow, and Taylor Branch, all of whom talked with me about the project, and especially to Julian Bond, to whom I turned frequently for help. I am grateful to Archie E. Allen for having the foresight to record John Lewis's life twenty years ago and for letting me use excerpts from those interviews now. I also thank Ernie Lofbladt of Magnum, who has never lost anything in his fifteen years there; David Perry of the University of North Carolina Press, for allowing me the freedom with which this work could flourish; and Alex Harris and the Lyndhurst Foundation, for believing in me and in this book. I want to acknowledge the great contributions made by my editor, Pam Upton, in improving and finalizing my text, and by Kristopher Hill of FinalCopy for setting it in type. Finally, I want to thank Guy Russell, my friend and the designer of this, our fourth book together.